ARCHONS, MIND CONTROL, AND A MOM!

A path to enlightenment!

by: A Light Worker named SKYE

ISBN: 1502791560
ISBN 13: 9781502791566
Library of Congress Control Number: 2014918358
CreateSpace Independent Publishing Platform
North Charleston, South Carolina

꙳ꙮ꙳

INTRODUCTION

Welcome. As I pull myself into the deep vivid memories of myself as a young girl, I recall often playing on this big hill across the street from the high school while my grandmother looked after me. My young mystic intuition gravitated peculiarly toward this one spot as if I knew where I was going and what for. The Alien Nurses, as they called themselves, seemed so fun and kind. I loved it when they came. I remember the energy. They would always bring me other kids to play with. We would play differently. We would go up on the ships, and they would take us up in these nice flowing parachute things. I couldn't recall much of what we did when we got to where were we going. What I do recall although is the one time they came and took us without a plan of ever coming back. I looked down at my grandparents from the parachute and the few others surrounding them all watching us. They were screaming at me to come back. I couldn't. The nurses wouldn't let me and the other kids out. I asked the nurses why as the others screamed below us. They were kind but persistent. They said it wasn't my real true family. I was confused. I loved my grandparents. They just kept taking us up. I looked down at my grandparents, after getting the DOWNLOAD report from the nurses. I recall telling them, "It has to be this way. You have to stop worrying!"

I recall a few years after this happening a vivid memory of a girl often coming to me. I couldn't to this day tell you who she was or where she was. I just knew I loved seeing her. She used to say repeatedly, "Do you remember a while back when the Aliens use to come and play with us and they took us?" That is all I remember. The only other thing I knew when the nurses took us is they messaged me to understand I was going to change timelines. It was my duty to go to another timeline because the timeline was in trouble. I was going to be replaced there, one day having my memory returning. My memory has been returned. That timeline is where you and I exist.

YOU AND I ARE GOD BEINGS. YOU, THE PERSON READING AND HEARING THIS RIGHT HERE, RIGHT NOW, IS A "GOD BEING" OF A VERY LARGE KIND. YOU HAVE HAD YOUR MEMORY INTENTIONALLY ERASED by energies controlling the hologram we have been trapped in here on planet Earth. Your perceptions of reality have been altered to wrap you into a consciousness that is not real. It has been a paradigm that has been installed upon you, giving you erroneous messages that you are anything less than the grandness of the "Godlike Beings" that we are. We are in a mortal hallucination, a virtual theme park, and who has control of the knobs is a question that everyone must face. You may believe I am coming to you with another sci-fi book, that you are to roll around the sheets with me in experiencing vibrant mystical intercourse, but I assure you this is far from any high-tech, made-up science fiction or religious babble to convince us of the fairy-tale, profound, happy ending that humanity is going to experience. No, this is far greater than hope. We, as humans, have no idea of the grand glorious lives we are headed for and how much of our memory has been erased…until now.

❧

My daughter's vibrant red golden hair flies across the halls of the Los Angeles Convention Center. Her inner heart is beating to the parallel outer pounding beats that endlessly pulsate the crowd during this weekend's electronic dance rave. Her half-naked body thrusts upward followed by the downward jolt to the floor one takes as the convulsions set in during one of the more intense drug overdoses. Although before her eighty-nine-pound, drug-overdosed body could fully come crashing down to the cold, wet floor smeared with the dripping sweat of the dancers, a bright light plunges itself forth as it rises up from behind the dark backside of MY body and gently roots its omnipresence above my third eye. Before I could truly set my eyes on what was in front of me for another second, without everything caving in on my heart, the heavy dripping of my tears were suddenly caught by its illumined essence as if it were the light of peace itself. Its warmth surrounded me. It was in front of my Altar. It was after it all settled in.

INTRODUCTION

A light so very powerful—it has ignited the memory within me that has been taken from you and me that recalls the time when we operated as supreme Godlike beings in civilizations such as Lemuria and Atlantis. Some of the "Akashic records" within me have been ignited as I continue to receive the downloads, feeling the memories flashing back through my life. In a splash my world is vibrantly altered when I was taken in a nanosecond and started to recall the essence of our supreme glory. I witnessed us overcoming such things as illness, disease, ill bodies, poverty, war, hatred, separation, and heartache such as we do. I recall the time we were extremely evolved beings that shared such things as free energy, telepathy, teleportation, and telekinesis. We operated as one divine being outside of the Matrix we are in now and expressed our individual grandness in multi-dimensions. The memories rush through the chambers of my heart, making a clear passage for the message to pump up into the veins of my head over and over, saying "We are Gods. We are Godlike beings. Why are we living like this? It, "the light," rapidly and telepathically downloads information into my being through its loving, peaceful presence of light knowledge or Light Being(s) as this presence is not limited. It holds me center. I pause.

I continued to watch as the light reaches out and catches not her body… but mine. It was my body that was caught as it was plunging to the floor, not my daughter's. My daughter's body made it to the floor after the energy that took over her body placed itself comfortably in a spot that caught not only her fall but also her life and has had an unknown departure date with free entrance. The "Archon," or the energy field being manipulated within her, has its own separate name to be identified as Taylor Brown.

Crystal meth with acid, crystal meth and alcohol and acid or meth mixed with Ecstasy is the cocktail question that has never been answered. It introduced my daughter's mind to the Archons and the Electronic Mind Control existing on our planet, which has induced several psychoses. Because of this it is understood that she has lowered the vibration of a part of her being to such extremes that she has opened a portal from our existence to another realm. It is believed the subtle energies around her delicate body (the ethereal) are being controlled without her, and other subjects like her, knowing it. An opening allows mind control or electronic harassment to take place through the Archon Network. A "portal of a lower kind" one believed to be under psychic control. Much of our very own shadow government plays a part that allows her soul, or the energies around her soul, to be mind controlled by a different one, and or controlled by them.

My mind continues trembling as I recall gazing over at my daughter in terror, observing her staring at the walls and laughing in a distorted manner at our first emergency room scene. The trembling within me ignites into full-blown anxiety now where I cannot catch my breath and bring the air in my body. It won't expand. I can't breathe. I could not get the air to come in. My trembling won't let me. The walls are spinning around, closing in on me, each wall I see coming in for the attack has a different outcome and not one of them is pretty.

As the light permeates my being to help me catch the breath and bring it back down in my body, it starts to download information into my own personal auric energy field through its warm, loving, and peaceful presence. I am starting to see more here than just what is in front of my own frontal lobe. I had started to catch sense of what was in front of my daughter Lara's frontal lobe as it took over the vibration in the room.

My eyes caught the glimpse of her body, as my own soul was trying to replace itself back in my own body. I was suddenly surrounded by a surge of utter darkness that captured the room as I watched it surround my daughter's essence giving me feelings of terror that I have never encountered. I thought that this dark feeling alone was horrifying enough, but when my eyes indeed steadied themselves upon my child's body, I became speechless. The nightmare began and the nightmare has never stopped. I will go into deep conversations with you of what that really looks like, what one really goes through.

If you are the parent of an addict and with mental illness, or, you or a love one has mental illness, I might tell you there is a little bit more going on here in the ethereal that we had no idea about. It is all winding down to the prophecies of our times, knowing all things will be revealed, knowing that grand information has been withheld from us as human beings—crucial information.

I was alone, a very young single mother in a huge city with no one. The subjects I had to touch and explore in my lifetime were far greater subjects than one frightened girl could figure out by herself. I had to touch the most frightening topics one would possibly want to face and with no greater pain than with her child. I had to face the Archons and everything that came with it. I was forced to deal with issues of psychosis, schizophrenia, brain chemistry, delusions, split personalities, 5150s (where you are taken on a hold for seventy-two

INTRODUCTION

hours in fear of endangering yourself and/or others), arrest, hospitals, medications, darker Alien races, rather than demons. Angels that are also known as extraterrestrial or higher dimensional beings, portals to other realms where the star gates are and what is happening since the quarantine has been lifted off of planet earth, the occults, the alien races our government has been working with, what races we are exchanging technology with in exchange for our children for hybridization programs, what races are capable of conducting such things as walk-ins and taking over ones soul, benevolent E.T. races, light-workers and how we are actually changing and assisting the planet into its prophesized Gold Age, the Matrix, and how to get out of it, not to mention the day-to-day heartbreaking scenarios that come to play when you are the parent of an addict.

I did not know all this was part of the awakening of the coded DNA structure that others also have had. I just thought I was taking my daughter to the hospital to get her help.

I care how you are affected in this world, really, I never knew how much I cared. It was the warmest feeling I had since my awakening and one I wasn't real familiar with. I cared that I had my dreams fulfilled, and I cared that my daughter was sick and I did have a view of praying for everyone around the world, but nothing where I KNEW WITHOUT OUT A DOUBT I WAS ONE WITH YOU, and it was time to go to work on the planet. I profoundly and suddenly had the need to give back to society in humble gratitude, knowing that so many before me gave so much, and it went unnoticed by me in many ways. It started to open my eyes to all the people who gave their lives or their time and energy so that I could in one way or another have a better life from the paths that they have paved. I took time to hold a moment of honor and acknowledgement for each soul whether I had known them or heard of them or not. There have been so many people, so many that have given us freedom by standing for a cause who were unjustly treated; it hit me hard. It also hit home.

My intuition was leading me more and more toward one day facing everything I had to face. It kept giving me ideas that I would indeed be writing about this. It just kept gnawing at me. I, on the other hand, had different ideas for my life. I didn't want to be the girl terrified to open up my heart and let gush out what I had been through and what was really going on, on our planet. I didn't want to take this role. I wanted it shoved under the carpet so I could hurry up and get on with things of my concern. How can I be successful? The thought of writing crippled me because I knew I would have to face everything if I wrote it out. My first scribble at the keypad was filled with terror. It was a clip that I actually kept of one of my daughter's many 5150s. The 5150, usually, it is seventy-two hours, but up to a month depending on the severity. Anything past thirty days is considered long-term treatment and is not the same procedure as a long-term facility. I recall running to the computer, opening up a "new document" page and started bursting out in tears that dripped onto my shaking body as I tried to explain the vast amount of things that were happening. Everything seemed distorted but very real and very raw. I was screaming at the paper, "I don't want to be in the position! I can't believe I am here now writing this, doing this. This is not my life. This is not where things were suppose to end up."

My encounter with the energy of enlightenment and the interpretations I started to get from then on is what has written this book. It also became clear to me that the spirit world wanted more than just my healing out of this and that it was far more than just my cry over my daughter. It became increasingly clear to me that there were parents of addicts whose child was also taken over by the Archon Network, MK. Ultra or Electronic Harassment or any of the fields the programming entails, and they didn't even realize. They just posted their child labeled as drug addict, mentally ill, or incorrigible. They, too, were suffering and being robbed of any normal life. Usually not knowing there was something more going on. Usually when a parent sees the child going crazy, at first, they immediately think it's a behavioral issue and they try to correct the behavior. Might we understand it is a far greater issue than this and the vast arrays of issues involved?

I, the parent, became lost in my daughter's illness. I don't care who we are or who or what we get lost in; lost is lost. For me, it was my daughter's addiction that threw me to my knees to a surrender so great that it brought me into the arms of enlightened states. This is a journey of enlightenment, one I believe you yourself may be embarking on. It is no joke being the parent of an addict and/or either taken over by the Archon Network. I want you to know that I believe YOU have been introduced and called to a course in Self-Mastery, whether conscious of it or not. Universal Law tells me that all souls seeking receive the same states of existence and the same knowledge of Enlightenment. Your highest self is aware of the intense journey you have been on. It has knowledge beyond what you could ever imagine. We are all in communication with that higher self and its interwoven web of supreme consciousness during this process together,

INTRODUCTION

including, even, writing "this" book. As you read this, creation tells me I am connected to the mind, our Oneness Mind, the Universal Mind, the same mind you are connected to in the ethereal that is sending out signals to me right now in my time frame, answering what you, too, are asking as you read this knowing you, the reader, are too included in this space as I am guided to do. There is no time in the ethereal world so it is important to stay away from any kind of logic where logic and time are not the same as what we know. Creation reminds me it is none of my business how it connects with another person. What is meant to be heard or not heard by another or how and what it means to that individual is a very personal thing between our Creator and that soul. I was to stay out of trying to figure out any other person's interpretation it has with another and just stick to the only thing that I will ever know and that is my own personal interpretation.

The deeper my daughter fell into the "Archon Network" the deeper the "light" and "Light Beings" connected with me as I have had a continued dialogue with this loving presence. The light presence walks me through a vast array of life's wondrous issues as my vibrant mind and open heart pours out its love for our sacred humanity. Falling so far beneath the levels of pain over my daughter's situation, what transpired was the recognition of our Oneness; and now, this was the only thing on my mind. So I set forth as such. I learned step by step how to handle the most torturous path one has to take. It gently calms my most baffling questions on how to cope with life being a parent of an addict facing electronic harassment with the Archons. The Archons have indeed truly started the invasion of earth in pursuit of an all New World Order. It continually reminds me of my mission here on earth!

Its essence calms the screams to the most intense esoteric questions about life and the Universe I reside in, whether it ignites the conversation or I do. It helps me understand the sacred timeline I am on and answers personal questions in life. Why was I born into such horrible conditions as a child? Why did I suffer violent abuse from my daughter's father? Why did I have the curse of raising this entity called my daughter who I loved so much?

The Light Beings explain to me I am a Light Worker, genetically coded to have portions of my memory returned to me within this time frame on our planet. These are interdimensional beings, extraterrestrial/Angelic beings of pure love. They have been in contact with hundreds of thousands of people now with the same information preparing us for the changes that are to take place here on earth (and within our government) for the return of our "Ascended Masters and Our Galactic Family," which we as humans will all be interacting with. As the light presence continues to send this message forth to me, you too will one day come to understand the same, as I am shown each soul will. We will one day recognize ourselves as light beings, glorious Godlike beings that have been trapped in a perception of separation that has literally manifested in the world. Soon, we will be seeing a massive upgrade in humanity. Our personal configuration to our DNA structure within our bodies are going to be returning us to our "Godlike Self-Beings" as we enter into the Golden Age.

If you are the parent, you, the parent, I believe, have signed up for a very profound soul mission that must be met in order for you to free one's self of the "ego mind" that has been intentionally induced for means of control to rob us from our memory. It is the sacred path one is on that cannot be omitted nor skipped. It is a journey and it is unavoidable. Each person on the planet will experience a path that will lead them to the death of the "ego mind"…this was my time.

A very loving message sent to me from the light is that a parent suffering from the effects of their offspring's situation is a strong clear unmistakable message that we are truly out of alignment with the creative source energy when we take care of others before we take care of ourselves. Taking care of one's self is a clear direct path to highest self. That energy surrounds us with the love and wisdom we will need to continue to send to the very ones we are seemingly destroyed by. These are the attributes that are capable to jet set us past such a horrific disease into the hearts of the ones we love and need to be heard by. I must state as directed: if my soul is not raised to the standard I am asking my daughter's to go to, that would be me appearing to control the situation from the outer realms rather than fixing my inner world, where, in fact, is the only place of true power. I do not know nor do I understand how anyone could call himself or herself a leader of something or someone and give orders unless they themselves have truly mastered their own lives. Unless they, themselves, have been through what they are preaching, they, in fact, are not a true leader, rather, just a preacher, and not many take to preachers. I find many try to run countries, cities, and companies without their own paths being mastered and there are whole systems behind these organizations cheering things on.

INTRODUCTION

One of my favorite passages in "ET 101" is when it talks about how many of our leaders are going to come to understand in a very profound way that you do not disarm dysfunctional behaviors until you experience them yourselves. This trickles down all the way to us individuals. I have no right to ask my daughter to shape up unless my side of the street is clean, which I find takes an enormous amount of tending to sometimes. We are fooled by how quickly the mind is thrown back into the illusions of the world, thinking it's time to point the finger at another as our poison rather than our medicine. Pointing the finger at my daughter Lara for my problem of me being out of control will not help me turn this into the magical path it was meant to be turned into.

Again, this is no joke. I have found my way presented to me through my personal spiritual experiences. The beauty on getting to such a level is how clear it has been made to me that we all can have freedom from the chains that are binding us to the hell we have been through with the people we love that have been affected by the Archon Network. My way does not mean it is "the way." It is "a way." I understand creation will have you take what works for you in my writings, and you will drop immediately what does not.

I suddenly started rising, before the sun came up, to write. The sun gently floats up to a beautiful rise right in front of the first place I lived in while writing this book, up in the mountains overlooking more mountains next to the HOLLYWOOD sign. Creative sources could not have placed me in a better space to write the first year and a half until I moved to a lustrous hidden site gently compressed in the corners of the peaceful Topanga Canyon, observing her utter beauty for the second half of the book. I thank Source with a commanding voice every single day of my life right now for the beauty that has surrounded me while writing this book. This is a practice I hope to never lose. Nature has surrounded me and nurtured me through this process as Source thanks me back in how it provides for me.

Until my awakening I never got up early. I would never even consider it. My clients in my healing massage practice are often entertainment industry people that never sleep, here in Los Angeles. I loved the evening hours over Los Angeles, later than most. In fact, when everyone is sleeping I can drive around Los Angeles and not be bothered by the traffic, making sure I am in bed in time for everyone to get up and start their chaotic lives and then go about my business when the majority is at work. In my earlier years, it would not seem unusual for me to be up early. Nowadays, all I do is cherish waking up early for sunrise and not to go to work. It is the Sun I am rising with. I noticed how my energy really changed and gravitated immensely toward the Sun. You may have also noticed this as a sign in your life.

Nothing could have grabbed my attention deeper and have been more profound in the deepest corners of my being than my daughter. You could have not gotten me any deeper. It was instinctual and it was to the core and it worked. I was so desperate for answers, as if I were the Buddha himself, starving to sit under a bodhi tree to find out how to overcome suffering in the world, as compassion melted its very essence into me. As if I were relating to other ascended masters starting from lowest earthly forms, eager to rise through every situation until finding the resurrection, I hated and despised my own suffering. Therefore, I hated yours.

I knew that the time has come for our planet to rise above the illusions of the world, which means anything that is not a message of love and healing will fall to the wayside. This is a very clear message I am receiving from Source and the Light Beings that must be adhered to, if we are to sustain as a species at this time on the planet. These catastrophes that are happening are going to continue to happen at even a greater degree if we do not, now, each and every person, wake up to love and disregard the illusionary world that separates us from Source and each other, including our galactic families. It starts in your very own heart. You, the reader, I am trusting, is at a highly evolved state just to even be drawn to this book, but also to realize the hell that the world is in and the devastating vibration it has left on our planet Gaia and how it has affected each and every person on her. You don't even have to be at a highly evolved stated to understand this. I say highly evolved because it takes a highly evolved person to really understand the depths of how we have been affected, controlled, and trapped in an illusion—a hologram, and who has control of the knobs is what we all must face. You must be doing self-work if you understand this. When I say "hell" I am not just talking about catastrophes. I am also talking about this in a literal sense as we are literally under a firmament, a gate that has been closed off from the higher beings in our vast galaxy, until now. Creator's message is that we were not meant to live in hell, even at such minimal levels and that a much greater state of living is now being called forth to our planet in general.

CHAPTER 1

THE CONCEPTION

The sun barely broke the powerful blue tones of our earth as it rose manifesting its light one shade at a time while I sat across an empty parking lot on this particularly misty morning. I feel my pregnant body tire more and more as I go from sitting to lying, waiting for my boyfriend (the father of my daughter-to-be and my usual ride home after my graveyard shift at a local convenience store).

Although in need of help, this was often a ride I did not look forward to. As I continue to fade further from consciousness a man pulled up alongside me offering an alternative option for me to have my ride home. Since the long awaited arrival of Lara's father was nowhere in sight, this seemed like a good answer to what was the fastest way back home for me to drop my tiring body underneath some warm blankets, the need for me to rest my body from the horrors I was dealing with at home. Experiencing profound physical abuse was at full throttle, gripping my attention much more than my reasoning of entering into a stranger's car.

My pregnant body repeatedly held embraced in a lock of unwilling surrender to perform whatever sexual act to ensure my body would be released to safety until the rush came. "The dark Aliens are on the planet," her father repeated as he would stare into my eyes and then stare into the fire alarm believing their presence was everywhere. The sweat would seep out of his body sending the broken down amphetamines seeping through the air throwing the chemical scent my way. Black rushes before my eyes before my ears can hear the ringing and I fly to the bed. The darkness seeps into the energy that surrounds the room and makes its stance as it hovers boldly over us. It becomes denser as it travels in from the porthole of his being that has been left open, unable to shun the vibrant chemicals of the crystal meth in charge of his actions. The door that allows the energy of the Archons to enter his own fragile mind, ripped open by anger, remained opened for them to be fed through my pain. My fear is their breath. They inhale the orgasms (the "life-force energy"), the very energy they need to climb the dimensional ladder. The life force that is sucked from our bodies taking it into their own being allowing the STD (Sexually Transmitted Deity, or "Archon") to become alive, to enter one's body perhaps even while the conception takes place.

I didn't want to fasten my seat belt too tight during the ride back to my house. I had waited so long for a ride and with the extra weight on my bladder I only found tightening it to be an irritation. Sinister vibes didn't seem to scare me when I wanted to get somewhere. I guess that came from my youthful (almost destructive) attitude that had yet to be tamed by wisdom.

As the ride set its place in motion, for some reason my hearing became distant as did my vision, almost as if I was becoming faint. Oddly enough, I was also becoming more and more shielded from the energy being sent to me from the man who was supposedly going to be helping me out. His energy was anything but pleasant. It was eminent of the horrifying darkness I was living with at home. Since this darkness had not come from its usual source, it was unfamiliar to me and had brought on a whole new set of sensations that I wasn't used to calculating.

I was fragile, at the depths of despair, and quite ready to succumb to any danger before me that would alternate between my hell(s), as my overall life or the "hell" in the moments I endured at any given moment. I did not have the energy to care that this man was sending such dark vibrations my way or that I had to fight off his perverse attempts to convince me to have sex with him while I was pushing his hands away from my breast.

My vision continued to seem faint. His words seemed to have drifted more and more into the fog as I am instantly but gently taken over by a loving powerful energy, a "wave of knowledge" if you will allow your mind, a wave that suddenly was able to transfer its substance of knowledge to me. Information, descriptions, thought forms, as if it was transmitting faster than any other information I was used to receiving. It is loving. It is pure. It is unshakeable.

THE CONCEPTION

This energy wave seemed like it took form; an Angelic being appearing before my third eye. Faintly and softly I see its female presence centering above my crown Chakra with features similar to mine. It was all as if it was in the imaginative world, and I was in touch with how very real that world was. The imaginative world is where Creator connects with us. Out of the blue I was somehow able to immediately hover over the frontal lobe sections of this man's brain. It was like I became part of him and my higher self was in charge of the interactions. I was feeling his energy as if **I** were inside his electrical energy field, just observing it, that's all. I was now seeing myself in danger. I knew what I was reading was accurate because of its speed for one (it's like every-thing is transmuted in a nanosecond, but very slow on the earth plane), and also because of the profound stance it makes. I was feeling the intensity and the urgency coming from this "vision" as if it was showing me the value in knowing my enemy (his darker side). The light was informing me to sense and understand the dark fields of energy that he was sending my way because it was about to manifest itself in the form of my physical death. I was shown that I had to exit the situation immediately and how.

Word by word I was directed on what to say as if I was befriending him knowing much about his life and who he was. I dictated. My mind took direc-tion. In a weird way my lower mind felt like I was appeasing him with words although wisdom took over and does not seem to advertise itself through me among people's very private conversations with their Maker. I do not recall the exact words I said. What I do recall is being taken back as if I were coming out of my intuitive trance into an awe of wonder watching this man surrender his guard and let me and my unborn daughter safe out in front of our home in Dayton, Ohio. It was the first time my spirit ever did anything like that. It was then that I knew this whole spirit world thing wasn't just something in my imagination(s) and my heart. It was my first real introduction as to what was to follow in my life until years later when I had my memory returned to me. It was way more than what I could ever imagine about the spirit world back then.

It is interesting how this little girl inside of me her whole life has had these bizarre events in which she would find herself protected and guided, and those mysteries started in my womb. I always had strong intuition. It was something I was just born with. Later, I found out how very much so. When she was born, after my thirty-three hours of labor ironically enough, it felt like

3

there were Angels there instead of anything dark whatsoever. And there were. They were all over. I had so much prayer and love around her. At that point, I was very much involved with spirituality. When I had originally met her father, before his meth addiction recouped itself, he was of clear mind and body and exceptionally spiritual. He read every spiritual and ethereal book there was. He introduced me to things I had never heard of. He was exceptionally highly evolved and aware. I loved his knowledge.

His profound and mysterious sacred geometry art paintings with women with their yoni open in shapes of squares and rectangles that all resembled something profound or scriptural, showed me he knew and understood what most couldn't. He was not afraid of death in the least. He knew that life was eternal. He excelled in his understandings of the Universe. I, on the other hand, grew up in a very right-wing religious small town and my Catholic school sheltered me from alternative views. Although when my daughter came into this world, all of my views changed. (They also changed when I was introduced to my first Al-Anon meeting in the very early 1980s and was encouraged to get my own understanding of God that worked for me and later, through me.)

Spirit gave this entity to me, I would always remind myself, especially when I doubted what I was doing with her and all the matters that concerned her. All mothers are carefully chosen by creation's own design, the body of our offspring miraculously comes through the womb of the mother. All fathers are carefully chosen as well. The musing of this being is dumped into the DNA of the offspring. What comes before us when we spread our seed to our little ones as they run off and spring has been much more than what I ever knew was in store.

Chapter 2

Getting Out

I realize now that the Angel wisdom being above me never left me. I also realize that all the spiritual groups I automatically started to gravitate toward had crept their way into my understandings of life and how I should be treated as a person. The deprogramming of my own dysfunction was taking place. Things that I believed were acceptable, with my older conditioning of being a subservient girl, were starting to be deprogrammed. We all have our deprogramming from the trance. Some are very deep, as I later learned, especially the ones taken deep into the occults. My real deprogramming came when I left the egoic mind (as I explain even further in the chapter on Enlightenment) and returned to being outside of the Matrix. I could not do that unless I started understanding the basics as well.

With the help of my Al-Anon sponsor and the girls in my support group who I saw all the time and became very tight with, I was able to take that little two-month-old baby and get out of the abusive situation for good. Once I had my daughter, it became a whole different ball game. Prior to the birth I could accept that he was abusive to me, but when I saw her in life form rather than in my stomach incubating I put a stop to it all. I was so thankful I had that shut off button and wished I would have had it earlier. There are woman that allow their offspring to be abused. It's the brain conditioning, the programming we are under in general as a society. I didn't know how I had that shut-off button though without my sponsor and the loving help around me. I remember the time that I went grocery shopping when my daughter was about eight weeks old. I came home and she was silent on the bed looking up with tears in her eyes. He told me he shook her really hard because she would not shut up. I couldn't let that go and shared it with my sponsor. She lovingly drilled into my head over and over that there was no difference between shaking a baby and taking a baby and hitting a baby with someone's fist. Abuse is abuse. I was sad that I did not realize the difference when she put it to me like that. Although how could I? I myself endured profound physical abuse when I was a child. This explains why I was drawn to someone who expressed love through control and violence. That's how love registered itself in my brain. My motive for sharing wasn't to tell on him. I wanted things silent and well. The program taught me I was going to be as sick as my secrets and that my secrets were going to keep me sick. By this time, I had a child I was in love with and caring for. I had no room to be sick and I really just didn't want to be anymore. Usually, it was hard to share abuse. You feel like you are somehow at fault. It is an odd brain-conditioning trap someone is under. There is even wiring of brain cells that feed off the trauma, it's like an addiction to the wiring that takes deep work to break. Once broken, a whole new world opens up. I left him immediately after that incident.

I had to start from nothing really. I was on welfare and had actually used them to get some schooling and food while I was pregnant. Actually, the welfare department in Dayton, Ohio, was great. They had you go to classes that taught you to believe in yourself and set goals. I still have the booklet and what I wrote. It stayed shockingly similar to who I turned out to be. I wanted a wellness center. Years later, I began a healing arts practice that has been in operation for over a decade now. I left then and never looked back. As sick as the system is that was the area I had used to my advantage. I was thankful I took myself out of the system as fast as I did. Today it is hard for me to accept the welfare concept for anyone unless it is urgent and temporary. Although knowing what I know now, I strongly state one puts themselves in their own danger being in the welfare system. The government needs us to depend on them, that is why they are in power. That is what is dangerous for us as humans, the people dependent on the system.

CHAPTER 3

THE LIGHT BEINGS DOWNLOADS TO SAVE MY LIFE

I wanted to know everything there was to know about life. I knew that I was one of the people on the planet connected to something very profound and very powerful and so very real. I wanted answers. "Why am I separate from you, God?" my pleading heart wanted to know. "Why aren't you here with humanity? Why is the world like this? Why did my daughter grow up in a world like this? Why didn't we get a chance to do it right? Why were the Archons invading us? Why was there evil?" I just wanted to be with Creator God after my very profound experience meeting the "light" and the "Light Being." I wanted all the answers. I also knew I was having a telepathic communication with intergalactic and or advanced beings and I had no idea it was all intertwined. My true Father Mother Creator God in heaven has indeed answered my many mystical questions as asked, and then some. I recall back to my childhood being from my tiny little very sheltered home town, where things were so very simple, where everyone remains oblivious to all this; I had had no idea I would be uncovering vast secrets about us human beings.

The following is how all the mysteriousness started to unravel:

The chains of hell bound me during my daughter's downfall. Shortly after her twenty-first birthday she had already been in approximately twenty-two hospitals, in and out of many prolonged mental psychoses, numerous arrests, several facilities, nine different homes, and years of destruction to her life and body. She is now considered gravely disabled indefinitely and sentenced to a lockdown mental facility for long-term indefinite treatment as she remains in the care of a public guardian, although her true guardian in this time frame is the Archon and the Archon Network that is basically in control of the Electronic Harassment here on earth. I have witnessed and walked through every waking moment of it.

When twenty-two years later (almost to the day), my surrendered heart stood before my altar 100 percent defeated from life and 100 percent defeated in my fight to help my daughter from her deathly addiction to crystal meth that had her into the arms of the "Archon Network," having control of the electromagnetic fields around her body, my only prayer now was that I would please not wake up another day and how can I set out to make this happen.

Instead, the Light Beings literally interfered. I wonder if it was the Alien nurses that intercepted. They knew I had a mission here. They made damn sure of it when they had me taken off the timeline where earth perhaps has already ascended. Perhaps they were in charge of something greater than I ever knew. They confirm this with me anyway. I think by now they have gotten used to me even questioning them.

This energy captivated my being, trying to get messages to me in its forms. It envelops my energy field. I stop moving as it begins to download its "light knowledge" energy into my being, again, giving me understandings of the universe. Understandings of life here within my being and life here within this time frame on the planet. I keep receiving the downloads as the energy flutters around me softly touching my face, to this day, almost every day. I can't get it out of my head; they continue to download me. You Humans are supreme Godlike beings. You lived in civilizations that did not experience illness, disease, ill bodies, poverty, war, hatred, or heartache as you do!"

The "Light Beings" are a derivative from God Source Energy. God Source Energy is the "Light." The "Light" was in my heart and mind so utterly peaceful. So peaceful I never wanted to seize surrender to it. I was at complete surrender, and I had no idea that this loving experience would ever appear to me like this. The noise all stopped. It had to. I was at the end. A form without form that was here among/inside my being now. I laid there in awe as the tears rushed down my face not knowing yet fully what was happening with my daughter. I knew although it was immensely serious for them to show up and insist on my learning's of the "Archons" and the "Archon Network infecting Gaia, our planet.

What I also became aware of is not only did I have a very profound spiritual "DOWNLOAD" or " AWAKENING," but it also became physical. I, of course, am in a human body remaining humble about my every day humanness, especially if my iron was or were to be low or if I am or have been somehow triggered by my daughter's situation and all that came with it. I notice changes when in my enlightened states. I no longer required the amount of food that I did before. I no longer required the amount of sleep I did before. My brain capacity seems to have increased whereas at times it is not uncommon to study two or three subjects or interactions in a single moment and understand what is needed from all topics. My intuition tripled as if there is no intuition, just conversations with the planet as if we were the only one in the dialogue. My energy became infused and remains with the mystical magical journey of our creation. It's filled with the wonder of the most fascinating realms of our existence, and let me tell you "Creator Source" is anything but boring. We learn the microcosmic and the macrocosmic of life, the farthest places in space all the way to the cosmos that line up equally in the individual human brain. We connect with leaders and masters from all of existence in all the vast Universe and Multiverse(s) and the intelligence in between.

There is no limit to where Creator Source takes you; that is, once it takes you. This, I found through my dying and what I call the death of my Lower Self. The death of my Lower Self has occurred because I literally died in a whirlwind of pain. I will remember for the rest of my life what it was like the days before my awakening. As I laid there shaking, sweating, in front of my altar it was like I was walking through the gates of hell. It was as if heaven was on the other side of hell and for some reason my soul went through hell first. I watched it as if I couldn't get to it. As if "me" was not there at all, the access to "me" was not in operation. I laid on the floor for what seemed like three days in a pool of sweating anxiety, as my heart would not stop pounding and my lungs longed for air. I couldn't breathe. It wouldn't come in. The air would not fill my lungs. I was serious when I said that my daughter's situation had literally taken my breath away. I shook in horror as my body was becoming empty without spirit. It was like I couldn't get to me. The only thing that did seem to remain faint and far off in the background was a voice. It was a voice that called to me, communicating to me that what I was going through wasn't real and that it was not the truth of my existence, even though my body was acting different.

A Light Worker named Skye

This voice, this intuition, kept a wire to me feeding me the same information: "It's not real. You are living in an illusion. Do not feed your enemy any longer. Your enemy is your illusion that you are separate from me. The food that keeps it alive is FEAR. You have kept your illusion alive but I tell you it's not real. It will leave your body and nothing unreal or unlike truth will remain in the light."

It felt real as I gasped for air. It felt real that I couldn't get off my floor. I was crippled in fear, unable even to walk to the toilet. The voice took over more and then more and then more as I started to listen to it, regardless of my eyes blacking out and not wanting to open to look at my world. I couldn't find "me" anymore. It was like I couldn't get to my essence.

I am convinced now when the Lower Self dies, the Higher Self takes over. Make no mistake. There is a Higher Self. There is a rebirth of self into the higher realms right here in our existence and right now. All things in life are cyclical. We are at a point in our evolution where the planets and our galaxy are going to be experiencing massive changes. Things we never thought were possible according to what I have been shown by the light. We are entering into a photonic age or a "Golden Age," the Age of Aquarius as prophesized. What is and has happened to me is happening to others. My higher soul literally "walked in" my body and took over, (I will further share of "Walk Ins" in a later chapter) setting fourth on its mission here and my life and everything about my life and therefore my life's purpose changed. Why wouldn't it? All I saw during my profound spiritual experience is that we were all one and we all had access to a huge kingdom; why wouldn't I want to spread the good news?

It is a process we are going through of breaking down the lower self of pain and illusion or lower based Chakra centers and entering into the higher realms of our existence. This is going on individually and on a planetary scale. Once this process takes place, the higher self has a choice to incarnate within the body. Once this profound exchange takes place, we use the terms like Higher Self, eventually ET, eventually Angel.

*It is important to mention at this point that throughout the book, I have chosen to use the~ symbol before the passages where I am indeed just the interpreter of information and the messenger rather than "me," the personality. There are two distinct forms of communication, as the higher translations are as I am doing just that, translating, not thinking. Sometimes it is very fast so I try to do as little editing as possible, therefore it is not always in proper format. This presence and this experience, as a whole, I find difficult to translate to our human conscious-ness through "words," as words have a way of using too much of the left brain's logical thinking where it ties you into your perception of a word. Therefore, the mind wants to analyze. Analyzing can be a distraction of the heart and complicates intuition and imagination where wisdom's essence speaks to us. Unfortunately, we are not, in general, evolved enough as a species to be able to communicate through much higher sources of communications than words...YET!

I cannot question this, as my logical mind lunges forward for answers. "Who do you think you are?," I say to myself, "to believe that the energy would appear to you in your life, defying the five human senses, announcing the sixth, and con-victing to a message of its love?" Especially with the life I have had. Its character makes no change as it never has. It doesn't care of my opinion of myself. It does not care how it appears to me. When it appears and pays no mind to the receiver's acceptance of it, it just IS. We know this from all great leaders with great messages. Knowledge and Creator Source arrives and only our brave great souls have come forth with messages standing before the people knowing of the ridicule, yet plow-ing full speed ahead, delivering messages our souls have bared witness to; messages to the answers as to how in the hell I was going to live another minute in my body, being the mother of a person in a deadly destructive situation that was killing ME; messages as to how I could pull myself out of the years of hell my life had been in; to literally walk from an emotional flat line into the arms of enlightenment.

The pain that I had gone through trying to manage the day to day life of my daughter's horrific situation forced me to such an extreme surrender that there was absolutely no place in my being that was not ready to take direction from the highest realms.

As I journey on I have learned that the only question I have to ask is not whether this is real but rather why I did not surrender earlier like I did. If I had had such knowingness of my access to Source, I would have never tortured myself for one minute thinking I was alone. I was tricked into believing that I lived in a helpless hopeless universe. This universe felt like it was me against everything else; me against the world fighting my daughter's situation and not understanding what was inside of her. If I had only known the truth that I was not alone, that there is a whole campaign of light working together for the supreme greatness of us all, I would have never felt so terrified.

CHAPTER 4

THE NIGHT SHE CAME HOME DIFFERENT

It's a fresh, clear Sunday morning as I rise to reach out and touch my day. Before I can do so my mind's memory scans back to the prior evening. I feel this sudden intense emotional jolt, recalling how I was observing my daughter's new mechanical behavior beating on the front door when she arrived home. I had excused myself from the lady to whom I was giving a spiritual/tarot card session so that I could rush over to see what was going on. The beating on the door stopped as my daughter powerfully plunged forward in a daze storming straight ahead into her bedroom, as I let her in. I tried to hide her vibrant behavior from my guest, although I couldn't help but notice that even a sweet kindhearted more mature woman, with probably more compassion then the average person, was taken aback as she politely planned her exit.

The prior night's events swirl around my mind as I move forward, noticing my daughter wasn't up and around yet. The spiritual group that I had regularly attended to that morning was a treat I had always craved. I didn't realize how crucial it was for spirit to have guided me there that particular morning. I also had had no idea that my entire life as I knew it was about to change. I was to not only have needed the armor from that morning's spiritual group; I needed all the spiritual armor I have ever accumulated over my entire life. It was a time that all the internal strength I had ever had in its full capacity was being called upon. It was a time every piece of wisdom I ever had acquired was powerfully being asked to come forth and take over my being, immediately. Although, before I could do that, my soul fell to the ground without my body when I did indeed see and look up at my daughter standing before me.

Before my eyes could actually catch a glimpse of her and as my dropping soul was trying to replace itself back in my body, I watched and I felt at the core of my being the surge of utter cold empty darkness that captured the essence around my daughter's body, surrounding me with a fright that I have never encountered. I thought that this dark feeling alone was horrifying enough, but when my eyes did indeed steady themselves upon my child's body, I became speechless.

The terror that I felt when I first saw my daughter's takeover, I have as of yet, struggled to find an accurate description for. A bottomless empty pit I see within my heart as I flash back to that seemingly eternal moment. It was as if life had given me a quick vision of eternity in some dropping pit that never stopped dropping. In that eternal hell I felt and I saw, with my inner self, everything my child was now taken by and it was not pretty. The dropping feeling was a falling feeling and an emptiness that felt like it went on forever. This feeling was so dark I actually had to leave the house. I had to get away from this unidentified dark energy and replace it with denial and replace it fast.

As I returned from my group, my child was sitting on the couch staring at the wall laughing. "Lara" I shouted, "what are you doing honey?" She continued to giggle at the wall in front of her. "Lara, what are you doing, could you please stop?" Now she was giggling at the wall as if there was a whole universe inside of it that she was observing herself. I continued to call her name from far off in her distance. Nothing. I got nothing.

My first reaction to place on top on my denial was anger. She's being defiant and she needs to stop this shit now. What the heck is up in her mind? She's floating around laughing when I'm trying to get stuff done. That particular day I was trying to get my band's profile, with our music, up on the Internet. I was always baffled by what a young computer genius she was. Her mind was clear. She was very bright, almost arrogantly bright. She was a very fast thinker, and when she knew her target, everything for her was full-speed ahead. I loved seeing confidence in her, knowing how sharp she was. She really did understand things at an expedient rate. You would also sense irritation from her if one did not keep up. She represented a powerful, petite girl with long, golden-red hair, porcelain skin, and blue-green eyes that immediately called you into her world.

A Light Worker named SKYE

She is an utterly beautiful girl. She turns heads everywhere with her striking, natural beauty. She was already doing some modeling here in Los Angeles and was very stunning at what she was doing. More and more photographers were seeing her, liking her work, and hiring her for jobs. Modeling wasn't her only forte. She loved to sing…loved it. She grew up listening to every song ever made of any genre and for endless hours she would listen, memorize the lyrics, and sing and sing and sing. She actually ended up in the studio recording songs with an all-girl singing group. Even before singing, though, I noticed her ability to dance. She was a regular dancer at Millennium, a well-known dance studio here in North Hollywood where all the major celebrities were known to train. She met and worked with so many other great dancers; some well known. She would often say, "Hey there's such and such on TV." She also shined at her drill team performances in junior high. Although, shortly after is when everything fell to the ground…and fell and kept falling.

My daughter continued to observe her reality. There was no chance of me getting in. Any attempt made by me to reach her in her world was not happening. I didn't know what to do, and this is something no pill, machine, or cast was going to fix if I took her to the hospital. I didn't know what to do. I was terrified when I got there. I somehow manipulated her mind to get her into the car. I ran into the emergency room and begged someone to come out to the car to get my daughter and help me get her inside. Something was terribly wrong. They would not move. I was shaking. I was frantically trying to get their attention. They would not come out to get her as I pulled close up to the door and ran in. The nurses' lives are at risk coming out to the car here in Los Angeles (or perhaps anywhere). At the Northridge Hospital they were not going to walk out and help me get her assistance. You have to enter the hospital with the patient even if you are on the curb begging for help. I ran out and drove my car up four long levels in the car garage while Lara floated along in her own world. When we got to the top floor, she started to realize she was at a hospital and refused to cooperate. I was frantic. I had to get her help. Again, I had to manipulate her to get inside. I had no idea how good I would get through the years manipulating her to get her to the doctor for treatment. It was a nightmare. I felt like I was lying. I wasn't. I was strategically planning. I slipped a note under the counter to the nurse stating my daughter is seeing things that aren't here. She looked at me and wrote down on her paperwork, "hallucinations." I thought,

THE NIGHT SHE CAME HOME DIFFERENT

How dare you write down something so weird about my girl! Then, I thought, Oh there is a name for this; hallucinations. For some reason I thought if there was a name for something, there was going to be an answer. That wasn't true. Although, the way she wrote it down it seemed like something common.

I recall every second like it was yesterday. We waited for the lady who was to do the evaluation. Once she arrived, we went into the room together to observe my daughter's distance from reality as her gaze stared over the walls in front of us while she continued to laugh. The evaluation was tough for me to watch. I recall leaving the room once while we were waiting for the psychiatrist to arrive. I stood at the end of the hall, setting my stare down toward her room. The lady from PET (Psychiatric Emergency Team) looked at me with a look I will never forget. It was as if she could see my future, and she knew it was not going to be good.

The first doctor came in to evaluate Lara. I remember it like it was yesterday. I remember the doctor's dark hair. She was Indian or Pakistani, very smart, and quite young to be a doctor but very astute. She said there is no way we can release her. As I drove behind the ambulance, I was a bundle of nerves watching my daughter screaming while she was being strapped down to the gurney to be transported to her first 5150 stay. It is something no parent should ever have to witness. Unfortunately, that was not the first ambulance ride I would be following in her life. My life changed drastically. I was terrified at the changes before me, though very well trained during times of crisis. Although, this was not just a crisis that needed some quick attention so I could hurry up and get my world back together.

The second hospital was immediately after her release from a seventy-two-hour hold. It was evident Lara needed to be right back in. This time it was much more serious. She resided at the UCLA Psychiatric Youth floor for a month. The doctor, who became the main doctor I was to get educated from, met me in the waiting room. He said, "Your daughter is very sick. There is a chance she may not continue on this planet anymore and if she does, she may not be normal." I can't tell you what that did to me. No parent should ever have to hear those words. It was beyond what you can imagine. The only thing I grabbed in that moment honestly was faith. Oddly enough, I didn't have doomsday in mind. I had maybe a bit of denial and a lot of hope. I don't know what made my mind reach for faith. There was no reason for faith to be there, but it was.

A Light Worker named SKYE

I had been around Creation enough in life to know that Creation was in charge and not the doctor, nor was I in charge. I brought my child home, very, very, sick. I recall scanning my backyard when everything set in. I saw that it all wasn't the same. It wasn't the same reality. The air seemed blurry and denser. I skimmed over my reality, almost as if I was on a timeline I wanted to ignore. I made a mental note of it to myself as I looked at the trees; where they were placed; and the yard; and how the grass grew.

There was quite a bit of brain damage to Lara. She was unable to function on many levels and it took quite a bit of care. We had therapy at the house nonstop, and I had to take her to places for treatment nonstop. It took so much to develop anything at all that would resemble functioning. It was devastating to my nerves, my energy, and my psyche. It was utterly exhausting. I still had to work. We had a three-bedroom home, a dog, two cats, a turtle, a huge backyard, bills etc. and I was the one making it happen. It is very difficult to keep it all happening especially when your spirit is not there.

Every time we (me and the treatment team) helped Lara back to something normal, she became normal enough to understand that there was a craving going on in her body that had no mind or care whatsoever for what she had just gone through. After all that, my daughter walked out the door and went directly right back to the one thing she remembered. Lara went on to use for six more years until she was to land in a long-term mental facility. She was mentally ill, on drugs, taken over by the Archon Network merged in Electronic Harassment and far beyond any mental reasoning over those six years.

CHAPTER 5

THE MOST CHALLENGING PART FOR THE FAMILY...

RECYCLING IN AND OUT UNTIL

THERE IS A BOTTOM...

Those six years were six years of utter hell for me. I am talking utter hell. If you are the parent of an addict with mental illness I do not need to tell you the day-to-day lifestyle of what a parent has to go through. Especially when the child is a minor. There was so much pressure. The pressure of being responsible, the pressure of fixing every single fuck-up she would throw my way, the horror of not knowing whether she was alive or not while I laid there in bed home alone, terrified someone had surely harmed her in her state. I used to lie in bed, hour after hour, waiting for the phone call from the officer that my daughter was dead. I laid there like that for one week one time while she was missing, running off on some drug binge. I hated the mental torture I was under. I never knew if she was alive out there or not. The only thing that went through my mind was more torture. If she was dead, I would say to myself that it was all my fault, because I really believed I had as much control as God. I have to work very hard not to play God of another and remind myself I am not the one who is in charge of life, and I am not the one in charge of death.

A Light Worker named SKYE

My daughter's Archon control merged with addiction has taken a toll on her mind and body beyond what I could have ever imagined; and so very fast. She had resided in a small apartment in downtown Los Angeles with rats, cockroaches, and dog feces. Her weak body does not eat. She cannot manage her mind enough to get to the food bank I have arranged for her when I am not there bringing her food from the SSI checks she receives for her disability. She has refused her medication several times, and when she does take it, she takes more than prescribed. I have no contact with her unless I drive down there, which I do almost every other day. There are no more cell phones to give her as they all have been pawned for drugs. The landline I installed had been eaten by rats in the building, and the management did not care to help because of her condition. There is no reasoning with her about anything because there is no mind to reason. To get her in the car to get her to a doctor was beyond what I could manage.

She eventually was taken in every other month on a 5150. The minute she gets out of the hospital she is found somewhere on the street acting in bizarre manners. Usually half clothed, wandering around with messy hair, a gazed, angry look in her eyes, stopping cars in their tracks to ask for either a cigarette or money. That used to make me cringe. She would always do it in front of our really nice place we had in Sherman Oaks at the time Sherman Oaks is a nice area of the Valley somewhat prime and well kept. I was so embarrassed, and of course, she stuck out like a sore thumb. Usually, the case was they would find her in the middle of the street, half or less than half clothed scrambling some nonsense out of her mouth. Her brain wiring was very messed up. Therefore, she usually had a difficult time getting out her words and she would often cross-reference words or just make up her own to try to communicate.

One time, I had looked my daughter's name up on the Internet. I noticed that she had been taken in by the Santa Monica police department at the McDonald's down by the ocean. They said in the report that she was on a substance that affected her central nervous system. It was apparent the damage that had taken place. I also recall the police officer at one of the final scenes before her long term care was to take place, where her psychiatric doctor had to call the ambulance for her to get her weak fragile body help. He had asked me if she was always this animated. "What do you mean?" I asked. I guess I had been

THE MOST CHALLENGING PART...

so used to seeing her abnormal I did not see how far she was off. He noticed her agitated twitch she had while rubbing her fingers together as parts of her body shook. The damage that had taken its toll on her frail eighty-seven-pound body was horrible for me to acknowledge, when, in fact, I did have the bravery to see it and acknowledge it. I seemed to have not noticed it because I didn't like that part. I didn't like that people looked at her strange.

Chapter 6

And Life Shall Reign;
Notes About The Indigo
Children

. . . I took a bath tonight. I mean I took a bath tonight. Tonight I didn't take a bath while having hundreds of worries to scroll through and make peace with before I resurfaced. I just took a bath. It is rare to just do something. I rarely just do things without worrying about my kid somewhere in the background. Tonight, I just took a bath. I washed myself and thought about me. I thought about my skin; how the water felt on my body as I played with its splashes. I felt warmth on my body. I felt the steam on my face. It can feel surreal to have moments of total freedom from worry, living with the constant threat of what's around the corner. I did know what was around in this case, and miraculously that warm bath remained a warm free bath.

Miraculously, I say here, because several months ago as a result of some odd behaviors, I learned that my daughter, in spite of her horrifyingly ill state of mind, was now bearing a child. I did not believe it when the father texted me the news. I said, "Oh no, not my daughter." Her body is way too sick to sustain a fetus. When I brought my own pregnancy kit to verify the news, I was shaking. My attempts to have her urinate for the test finally succeeded. "There is life here!", I trebled aloud hugging my daughter in tears. Regardless of the situation, it felt special because it was life. It was the life of our Creator, an offspring of prime creation. I stayed in that moment and gave my daughter a hug confirming that there was indeed life inside her. We had a special moment together. My next immediate instinct was to get her to the doctor because her and her boyfriend's choice was not to abort.

My honor for life was met with reality. I also had such mixed feelings about this pregnancy. I've sat day in and day out before my altar. I've laid in bed countless nights praying to the cross that's overlooking the mountains on Cahuenga Blvd. (Ironically, that is also a supposed secret holding place for the phallus of Osiris). I gaze at the cross from my big windows here in the Hollywood Hills. "Please, heaven, help my daughter. Please, God; any God. Please, Creator. Please, Source, help my daughter. Please, Buddha. Please, bring "help." Please...I wasn't thinking anything like "BABY!" I was honestly just wanting to wake up and have it all gone. I couldn't even wrap my head around this. I recalled going down to bring her food one day as she was sweating, lying on her bed. She had been lying there in that apartment this whole time under those horrific conditions with rats and cockroaches and dog feces with a starving body and a baby inside her.

I had to step back and let the Holy Spirit do its work with this new child so bravely coming into this situation. I believe this child entering this planet at this time frame under these conditions has a very special mission.

I still whirled the situation over and over in my mind as I continued to flutter around Los Angeles from appointment to appointment thinking in my car. I could not, for the life of me, understand why this soul would be born to such conditions. I shake my head again but the same reality exists. I still try to somehow see if I can bargain with this little guy, "Hey, kid. You know you can still go back to God? You're not here yet. Please don't do this to yourself." I've had to repeatedly calm down from several anxiety moments I've had, wondering what kind of life this child may have.

I fretted over that because I somehow felt responsible for everything. It was like being the matriarch of the whole thing. I was becoming a grandmother, not just a mother. My already strong maternal instinct felt like it had to watch everything with the little chicks in the nest. I had this idea that because they were mine and not God's, that I was responsible. I deemed the soul of God within her incapable of drawing to itself the exact conditions it needs to bring to itself, for the exact agreement it had with the Creator higher soul, to do what it needs for its ultimate highest good. I had found myself constantly undermining the Creator, constantly thinking I am in charge of another's soul, constantly thinking that the only way their good is going to come to them is through me. How egotistical! This might be a good opportunity to introduce to you the new souls that are incarnating on our planet now.

A Light Worker named SKYE

NOTES ABOUT THE INDIGO CHILDREN

*Our newborns will have a much clearer idea of truth and how to utilize it. Infants are in the greatest command we know. They are real. They authentically express their needs, untainted and unfiltered by thought or the Matrix. They are coming from spirit world. They are used to much higher vibrations, and their spirit has been traveling at much faster speeds. They get cranky fast, being so constricted here (and they let us know it) in their new physical bodies. Once the child is born and subject to such denser vibrations, it slowly loses sight of its ability to "use" such high-energy attributes, as we all once did, by expediently manifesting the energies and structures around oneself according to what is needed. That is the world we are now calling forth one by one. One soul at a time will now be awakening to an enlightened world we are approaching. Usually, through grave heartache, one finds its surrender. This is our time of the coming of light. Now, on the planet, we are paving the way for a much higher consciousness; the Golden Age; the Aquarius Age that has been predicted. The vibrations of beings coming in and being born are much higher than what we are used to; so much higher that the core of our fundamental thought systems, as we know them, must prepare to be shattered in order for the resurrection to occur. I am grateful for the new onset of the new babies, for they will carry with them much more light and knowledge. It is going to be much needed. There is a new set of children that are incarnating on our planet known as Star Seeds, Indigos, and Crystal Children. These babies born in the last decade or so are highly evolved souls that have not lost their memory. We are indeed headed for something magnificent. These souls have extreme knowledge of the higher realms. The earth condition of a human is unlike theirs. They are very advanced souls!

In spite of my genuine need for answers, Spirit boldly reminds me to stay out of its plan with another. That did not go over to well with me. I think it should have been up for discussion. I am part of this. I am the one who has lived through this day in and day out with no break until now, and now the thought of more work after the life I have had seems so unfair…yack, yack, yack my mind goes, and you know what happens then. I suddenly feel peace! I feel peace! I cannot understand why now, but every time I think of this baby, I feel peace. I just stopped questioning it. I began to step back and be in awe of Creator's plan for life and be in even greater awe of its command!

CHAPTER 7

PUBLIC CONSERVTOR, LOSS OF FREEDOM, LOSS OF RIGHTS, LOSS 0F FAMILY

The apartment manager, where Lara had been residing, was looking toward me nonstop for answers on what to do with Lara, and she was not nice about it. Lara would intrude on everyone in the building by pounding on their doors until they came out as she was asking for cigarettes or money. I am surprised they didn't shoot her. I am the mother. Therefore, I should manage this was the message I kept getting from the manager named Sandra. I want to take a minute to run with this because it is important. Just because I have the title "mother" does not mean that I am responsible for life. I am not. I can't be. She is her own separate person. I don't know why everyone expects the parent to work it out, but they do. Even her being over twenty-one, people still believe I should be a magician. They do because they are ignorant. That lady that managed the apartment literally used to say to me, "Well you're her mother. You're the one who is supposed to take care of this." I wonder if she thought for one minute that I couldn't. Everyone just thinks, "problem...parents," like I could change it. It was like telling me that the sky is not behaving right therefore this blue color that it has should be changed to orange, and I am the one to change it.

Seeing my little baby girl like this, the little baby that I used to hold in my arms and treat as the most sacred being alive, now, in this condition, just killed me inside. I went back and forth in my mind into the deepest darkest corners with Creator God and had to face how sick she was. I had to face the serious fact(s). I kept wondering myself if this girl is beyond repair. I had never seen a drug addict so sick. I had heard from the sergeant at the North Hollywood Police station that Lara was one of the worst cases he had seen.

Lara was so sick. I just kept asking myself over and over how she was going to make it. How can a brain and body this damaged repair itself? How could she possibly rebuild her brain and all those damaged cells? I just kept wondering if she was damaged goods and was just going to drift into death. I recall my spiritual advisor saying to me that God was in charge and under God all things were possible. I recall taking a moment and surrounding myself with this thought. In fact, that's all I had.

Every time there was a 5150, it made me irate, because a 5150 was all there was. You could get your child help to get them stabilized enough to go right back out again and continue what they were doing that got them there. It was insane. It made me crazy that they could walk right out. Many parents struggle with this here in California. There was nothing I could do. If she was not willing, no one was going to keep her and continue treatment against her will. No hospital here will cover the expense. Even if they did, she was not going. I had begged doctor after doctor to keep her. I needed something done. It was awful feeling so helpless. There were so many 5150s, and it wasn't getting any better. Finally, after I had begged every doctor in town and called every agency and mental health program to get help, I met Dr. Ramirez, who was the main doctor to see her at UCLA. UCLA is one of the best treatment centers in the country when it comes to this stuff I had heard, and I could not have agreed more for many reasons. I later found out WHY it is one of the most profound hospitals on this subject based on remarks from the experiences of Susan Ford/Brice Taylor, and its far greater than I ever imagined, and it's not just for their brilliance, as I later explain the truth of what is going on with mental patients!

Rev. Carrie was a wonderful spiritual leader that I had been working with at the time when Lara first overdosed. In fact, her sermon was the one I went to the Sunday morning that I witnessed the takeover of Lara. Rev. Carrie really encouraged me to get my daughter there. She had quite a bit of education in this area, and I was very thankful for her recommendation.

Dr. Ramirez had called me and we had had a wonderful conversation for a long time. He made it a point to tell me that he actually took the time and looked at Lara's entire history and saw that the last twelve months of her life she had been in the hospital on 5150 eleven times. There was one time she got out and two days later she was found on the street in the same condition. Dr. Ramirez was the first to take the time to notice. He couldn't help but see the state she was in; even once she was stabilized, she was unable to care for herself whatsoever. What also needed to be taken into consideration was, of course, the pregnancy. It was the ticket that got her attention. I understood that this soul heard my desperate call for help and fully understands what it is coming into. Knowing this experience is exactly what its personal soul needs in order to play out its own karmic path. It now became two lives that were going to be greatly affected. The life inside of her, in this dimension, had no voice that we could hear. My view zoomed into this new unborn baby thanking its essence for coming to the scene and getting my daughter noticed. At this point, I started my immediate communication with this new soul to be. It was like I received the download from his soul to mine. I understood the purpose. Esoterically, I became in tune with this soul. We started a private dialogue.

The doctor asked me if I had ever heard of conservatorship. I was familiar with it. I was also terrified of it. It meant she would have her civil rights taken away. That was a big deal. It meant that I had to be responsible for quite a lot more than what I was already subject to. This whole thing had gotten me so far down the emotional hill I was barely breathing. I would long for air but my lungs would fill up with anxiety. I was emotionally and physically whirling in my own pain over this. I knew without a doubt that if I did not stop, I was going to stop my life on this planet.

I made a huge decision to have the State of California assign my daughter a public guardian rather than her own mother. I believe I was divinely guided into making the choices that I did, for many reasons that were about to unfold. Nonetheless, it was something I anguished over. I was trying to get her in a facility for long-term treatment. I knew that the public guardian could help get her in and keep her there. I learned that many parents purposely give up conservatorship because it is better for the child. The public guardian can actually get my daughter a bed faster than a multimillionaire. I have seen it. It's part of the plan. It is also better for the parent to not make such harsh decisions for their child. Some mothers can't do it. They get their child in there and because they are the conservator, they get them out once the child begs. It is hard to see your child in a mental institution. We want to bring them home and have all the pieces back together. I didn't know I could give in. I thought I was just supposed to go until I died, being her mother, trying to save her. Although, for the first time in my life my body said, "No." I couldn't breathe. I had to stop. Life made the decision for me.

I was gleaming with hope and relief. I tried so hard for so long to get this girl help and to no avail. When she was a minor I had no option whatsoever to keep her in treatment. If she wanted out, then she left. At least, as I mentioned, that is how it is here in California.

My elation for Lara getting help was quickly hammered with the next set of events that, to this day, cuts as deep as a cut could go, even with all of my spirituality. I anxiously called to hear my daughter's voice and to hear that she had been transferred from UCLA to La Casa ok. I continued my efforts to reach her and was starting to get concerned. My emotions were all over the place. I felt guilt for having her be with a conservator that wasn't me. I felt scared. I felt anxious. I felt relief. I had nerves all over the place, and I also felt disbelief. It seemed like a long period of time from the transfer to the time we had spoke. It felt odd almost like there was a whole period where I had no access to her. It made me exceptionally nervous.

Prior to the hearing, I had a wonderful visit with my daughter. Though in a raging state of mind, she delicately said to me, "Mommy, you will never let anyone take me and become my parent will you?" I held her and said, "Of course not, Lara. No one will ever take away the fact that I am your mother and I will always be here for you, honey. I will never leave you. I am your mother." The next vibration of my daughter and I was in the courtroom, agreeing to have my daughter be assigned to the State of California. I can't tell you what that did to me. Everything was happening so fast and there seemed to have been no time for me to process the magnitude of it all, it was all about taking the next right action. I loved my daughter and I had to do whatever she needed. She needed help beyond what I could give. There would have been so much to deal with, and I could barely function. I was taking tons of pills, either to sedate myself or just have my emotions come up to a normal state. They probably kept me alive. In fact, to this day, I am convicted that is what helped keep me together, ironically enough. I was also drinking tons of wine. I look at that and think, "Oh my God. I am the one who could be dying of an overdose trying to manage someone else's overdose." It wasn't until I got a DUI myself that I paid attention to the destruction I was doing to myself. Before my awakening to Spirit, I had gone through stages in my life where I was somewhat heavy into drinking or taking sedatives, but the difference for me is it has always been a stage. When it's done, it's done, and there is no craving something different or wanting more. It was simply not an issue when I was done, and life went on as normal. That did not mean to me, though, that because I wasn't addicted to chemicals that I didn't have a ton of work to do on myself.

I recall running into my counseling sessions with my spiritual practitioner, David C. He heard everything I was going through and still does to this day. He remains very close to me. This was too big for me alone. He walked through almost every step of the way with me. He was definitely my voice of reason. It was all based on a solid foundation with Prime Creator and a very solid setting for me to get out of my heart everything that was aching.

I knew that I had to release Lara to the State, and it killed me. I was also told by the doctors that I was to have a grandparent's right to this baby even if there was a conservator; if they only knew what I was to experience with "THE DEPARTMENT OF CHILDREN AND FAMILY SERVICES." I will tell you that they are anything but a family organization. It is inhumane. It is a clear-cut case of the Illuminati and the Illuminati control (much like everything else is nowadays here on planet earth.) Illuminati, basically, to recap in general terms, this is very general, are the secret societies that were originally formed after the death and supposed resurrection of Christ. They held hidden knowledge that had to go underground to be preserved due to the churches and elites wanting control. This great wealth of knowledge had to be protected. Eventually, some of the Illuminati divided and hijacked the cartel of hidden knowledge and mingled with the churches, elites, banking systems, and darker entities becoming corrupt, effecting every human right and government organization we have, including, "Children Services," aka DCFS, and the Vatican as later I will explain in detail.

I was still getting concerned that I couldn't reach her. Part of the reason I said to myself is I am sure it is because of her pregnancy. Most of the time, she is sleeping. The father of her baby complains of the same thing. It's hard to reach her. I waited to hear her voice.

A Light Worker named Skye

The first time she answered the phone in a seemingly agitated trance, as I started to explain my stance as to why I could not be her conservator. The only thing she said to me in a stern, straightforward, seeming trance is "None of this matters, Skye, and you are not my mother." The next thing I was confronted with was my daughter being in a full-blown psychosis. This was a full-blown break where (I will fully explain later) the Archon Network tweaked her relationship with her family through the electromagnetic energies around her body being controlled by people (Controllers) and experiments running her mind. This energy took over her entire being and to this day has not left. "**You are not my mother!**" This was the only reality she was persistent about, whether it was done in an aggressive manner or compassionate manner. YOU ARE NOT MY MOTHER BECAME HER REALITY!

I can't tell you to this day what this has amounted to. How dearly this has affected me to my core. Not only was this devastating to me, her dissociation with her family terribly affected her baby as I will share in later chapters.

Shortly after, I am on the phone with Lara's conservator or public guardian. This did not seem to help much. I am learning more and more what it really means to have your daughter taken over by the state, with her civil rights taken away. I am her payee on her SSI account, and I am now instructed to turn over all her money. If she has a phone bill due or needs to clean up a few things she owes with that money, they do not care. Lara's conservator informed me that even if Lara had a car, they would come in and take it. They sell it, and any money goes to her rehabilitation. They also came right into her apartment, declaring everything she owned to be thrown away. I didn't know they had such rights. Every step of the way seemed like another dig. Did they not realize there was a real person there that had clothes, pictures, childhood memories, and other precious things we had both gotten together in life lying around there?

The conservator blurted out of his mouth that they (people like Lara) lose their rights when conservatorship is taken over them. "She is the property of the state," is the message. He must have a lot of his cases where other people are aggressive with him by how defensive I felt he was. I want nothing but treatment for my child, but it does not take away from the fact that this hurts like hell.

The first call I got from her (now) new public guardian was that she tried to jump over the fence of the institution. I panic. I keep going back to the moments when she was a little girl and we can make it all better. I want to bring her home. I want to start all over.

Initially, Dr. Ramirez and I were working very hard behind the scene to arrange everything and how it was to go down. He explained everything to me. Lara was going to have a conservator who was named Lewis. Lewis explained everything to me, and it was quite alarming. I didn't realize the power they had and how abrupt they were about it; so much to go over with him and how it would take place. Nevertheless, I went with the flow. He kept me somewhat secure, although his role was quickly taken over by a brand new person, and the thread of security I had with Lewis ended up being quickly replaced by the new guy to the scene, Brian. I did not initially know there was going to be another guy and eventually yet another, then another, assigned to the case as I now see the procedures are with these organizations. You get an initial person as an intake, go over the entire thing and pour your heart out, only to have your paperwork transferred to the next person you don't know to go over all your exceptionally personal business with. Lara was to be placed at La Casa here in Southern California. This is a wonderful facility that works with gravely men-tally disabled adults. It has a great reputation from most, including the patients. The patients tend to like it there. They are very good with them. I learned so much from how they handle situations. Ironically enough I had also learned how they worked with patients through Lara's father. He had a period in his life where he was a resident there. It reminds me to remember genetics, even the genetics of crystal meth. This was always something I had to consider. He later in life would say to me his own mental disturbances were all crystal meth. "It's all crystal meth," he repeated over and over. Crystal meth aka "The Devil's Drug!" I later learned of the profound connections between crystal meth users and the Archons!

There have been staff members there (mainly Mioki and especially Katie) who were just like Angels to me. I felt so safe when I had expressed my full gamut of emotions and I was always clued into how Lara was, as agreed on the initial paperwork. They were wonderful about it. Some places are not like this, and it makes it much harder on the parent. I was so thankful for the warmth.

CHAPTER 8

DEEPER IN THE ILLUSIONS, PHYCHOSIS MERGED WITH D.I.D.

(DISSOCIATIVE IDENTITY DISORDER)

Since Lara has started her long-term treatment, the Archon or electromagnetic energy around her body being controlled or manipulated, decided to take over on a massive scale. The Archon Network which I will fully explain, for now it will represented separation from Source allowing oneself to be controlled by outer negative forces. She had done so much damage to the vortexes (or the energy centers pattern around her body) with the drugs that the hole in her auric field was wide open for the Archons to take over. They take over, and their leader, if one has a controller, calls the shots through the Archon or Leech attached to her. Most are controlled through implants connected to a main AI, or Artificial Intelligence, which in general takes over the trance. Many, many people are controlled by the AI in such subtle ways to begin with that they don't even know it. I will further explain.

"They are in control. The Controllers of the planet!" Lara, as I repeatedly mention, often would call them "The Law." She says they are the Rulers. She in short has told me that they are from Mars, they are a family, and one day they will return. This is true. Actually on the benevolent side as well as with the controllers. Both. I believe in more than one alien race that we hear of that is from Mars is not hostile. In essence, the Archon or energy inside her, could be an attachment to a version of

DEEPER IN THE ILLUSIONS, PHYCHOSIS...

her multidimensional self where she existed on planet Mars perhaps even in peaceful territory, perhaps when indeed in history their civilization had to leave Mars and come to earth. Either way she had a view of another version of herself. Or herself was under a Mind Control.

The Mind Control that takes over through the Archon inside her is very persistent in its reality once it takes over. Depending on the Archon and its reality, Lara will hold it for several months or even up to a year, as I have witnessed. The Archon energy will drift in and out of her alternate reality spaces depending on what her mind can hold in her normal state. I noticed when agitations are high, so are the delusions and the Archons, or the electronic harassment is in full bloom. In this particular takeover, as I stated, she refuses to acknowledge me as her mother. The Archon inside her, and or her handler, as I explain further in the Archon Chapter, or the energy controlling her around this planet, has a mother and father in the ethereal. She answers to that, not me. In fact, when I speak to my daughter, she tells me she is going to get into trouble from "THE LAW" for speaking with me. She tells her boyfriend the same thing.

Dissociation from one's self (DID, dissociation identification disorder) such as what my daughter has experienced, is the mental torture they, the Controllers, inflict as well. I will further explain in the Mind Control chapter. It is interesting to note many of the pop videos, not just Britney Spears, are shown having secret clues in them by putting Manicheans next to them. This resembles the machine like person. The machine like person that has a controller or a handler.

This whole Archonic Network has invaded our land. And yes as Laura Eisenhower stated, "The alien invasion has already begun," in her interview with Alfred Weber. She has a wealth of information on the Archons. This whole operation with the Illuminati in general is believed to be why many celebrities have been either killed as we hear (Michael Jackson, Whitney Houston and Tupac) (in some form or another) or some of them went crazy, like Britney Spears whose clone was made to watch these videos of these horrible Pickford murders over and over according to the interviews with Donald Marshall. That is why she had that mental break at the time she did. Tila Tequila will confirm all of this as well. She survived this and has come out like Donald Marshall to inform us. Again, as I mentioned, the only reason I personally am mentioning these names is because my daughter would constantly tell me they had Britney

Spears there. There, in the secret place where there is communication in the ethereal between these celebrities and or there colons or there ethereal body that is all under a form of Mind Control operated under our shadow government, as we have found out. I was of course floored when I put all the pieces together. They take beautiful young pretty girls, especially in the entertainment business. Lara was up and rising in her own way as I explained in the beginning; she was definitely gorgeous (that's the main pick, young and beautiful). I will also bring up David Marshall later on as well, as his information will validate much of the rest of this book.

My daughter will look me in the eyes, in a very private room searching the very private corners of her mind, and tell me I am not her mother for about a quarter of the time of our fifteen- to twenty-minute visitations. At first, I thought she was acting like that because of some internal anger she may have about me not taking conservatorship of her and having the state send her there. I had given her space to process that, but for the most part, there wasn't much time for me to engage the "new parents" that she now claimed she had that wasn't me, referring to one of them as "Daddy or Doo Doo! I had not really even had the chance to process all that, my mind was much more geared to having her focus whatever doses of reality she did have in our dimension on the growing baby inside her.

I met with her social worker from La Casa in Long Beach, California. We had had great conversations on the phone, and I was excited to see her. I am always thankful for anyone who helps my child, no matter who it is, or where they come from. Lara is pregnant. She is going to have her baby while residing in a mental hospital. She was using hard drugs during the beginning of this pregnancy. There was no mind-body connection. What was happening inside her body appeared not to be registering in her mind. Detached from her mind and detached from her body, I sit and watch my daughter fall deeper. It's hard to see. She was formed and growing inside my body for nine months, and I took such good care of her. I protected her incubation period. I had this internal pull to stay purified during my pregnancy. "Why didn't she have this?" I had always wondered.

The courts have taken her in their care and find her unable to care for herself. She is in and out of mental psychosis, sometimes with an Archon controlling the situation and sometimes with the psychosis controlling the situation with the electronic harassment, one feeding off the other. She has breaks from our reality; breaks from our world and connects to another. Although, how I see the world, I wouldn't mind the connections to other worlds if they were, indeed, nice healthy connections, perhaps like to Prime Creator.

Lara's illusions and takeovers have stayed strong in length and strength. The delusions are running the show in her daily life. In her first takeover, she held the delusion that she was engaged to a man who was never there. She did meet him. She did date him, he did seem to care somewhat for her when I saw them arm and arm, face to face falling asleep, but when he left, she, in her mind, did not. She told everyone that she was engaged. She said she had conversations with him. She did not. She said he came over. He did not. She said he was away, tied up in jail for something and coming back for her. He was not, not that I knew of. She would even run around in a happy state of bliss talking about him. In fact that was the first break, literally, a break. When the father of her baby met her, he said that is what she repeatedly told him. That was real to her; she had tattooed his name on her back.

The second set, the "you are not my mother" set of illusions, or disassociations—when I looked back at it all, I realized that these disassociations were perhaps defined more with the Archon behavior or electromagnetic energy disassociating her from her normal reality into a different one (further explained in the MK ULTRA chapters) rather than just the psychosis or a delusion. They hop between dimensions. Although, as a side note, Lara, opening the portals that she did, may have had true insight into other dimensions. I also understand that the Archons bring confusion and hatred to Light Workers like myself. It is literally their job. The Archon inside of her will go out of its way to bring confusion and hatred to the ones who love the soul.

There was also an incident that actually happened more than once where she insisted that she and her boyfriend had had five children and they resided with them at their place, in their home. She got very angry with me one time when I brought her home to her apartment that she insisted wasn't hers. She always talked about the children. This was before she was pregnant. Perhaps she truly was tapping into another dimension. I cannot be honest with myself and call that a delusion. She did, indeed, later have a child. I do not know how many she will end up with, but she was in a reality where there were five.

A LIGHT WORKER NAMED SKYE

Yes, those are the cards on the table. I am sharing my life with my daughter, my daughter's delusions and my daughter's Archons and treble watching the electronic mind control! I have had many conversations with the Archon inside her. It is profound, at times, the information that my daughter has coming through her. I learn quite a bit from her, and from the Archon(s), Archon Network, inside her. Equally as much I then, of course, was introduced to the Archons right here, right here deep inside and on our planet merged in our minds blindly wrapped in the Matrix. Blindly wrapped in our egos and the egoic mind is what Source directs me to explain through the "LIGHT BEINGS" in my very first translation of them, (translated further in part three and in the Enlightenment Chapters), as it spoke loudly to and with us about earth's condition!

CHAPTER 9

COUNTINUED DENIAL OF HER FAMILY;

REJECTING CONSERVATORSHIP

What I did not know at the time was that once I gave up conservatorship that it would be a nightmare for me year after year to ever recapture it in Lara's condition. After one year the conservator always has the right to go before the judge and ask to get off conservatorship, if a person proves well enough they have the right to have their public guardian removed. I have stood in the courtrooms several times to try to attempt to regain conservatorship of my child, although this one particular year I was so mentally torn apart on the following procedures, I have documented them in real time as life was happening then.

Tomorrow the judge on her case decides whether she is gravely disabled and unable to care for herself or well enough to continue on with her life without a conservator. If she continues on with conservatorship the one right she has from what I am told is to request who would be her conservator. In other words I was told she has the right to deny me. Her present conservatorship is over at midnight as I sit here on my balcony overlooking the mountain watching the sunset. This particular sunset is with the Venus Transit. I have sat here in prayers and chants for the last three hours as the sun melts down over the mountain. I pray for guidance that I am doing exactly as spirit and Mother Love would have me do for the highest good of all concern.

A Light Worker named SKYE

It was a tough decision going back and forth to consider having my daughter back under my care. I was tormented with my emotions not knowing what to decide. What I did know though is that I would be guided. With the extreme complications concerning the baby to be, I was very driven to take this situation back under some control, I also wanted to stop enabling Lara's psychosis about me not being her mother. The further she fell into conservatorship the further the psychosis went on that I was not part of her life. The treatment team suggested it would also be a good idea for me to conserve her. I, on the other hand, took a huge breath and started doing some investigation. I read all the laws concerning my responsibilities and felt much safer. There are definite means of protection for a conservator if something were to go wrong while she is under my care. There are also all the resources I need to assist me. Prior to her initial conservatorship, I was in no way in shape to take this over, I needed every break I could get. I could not lift a finger to do one more piece of paperwork, not even to find this information. Today much has changed. I have a huge team of help behind me. I do not know if my daughter will detest me, though these last couple of months we have gotten closer. But she still will fade fast into "you are not my mother, Skye" when the issues that are around her get deep.

I have a little video of me and her being a touch silly right before the hearing of her acknowledging me as her mother. It was a moment of a breakthrough. We were in a good place and having fun. I also knew that her having to face a judge to let her know she is gravely disabled is not something her inner being may want to like to hear. When she is losing control, she will go to the only control she has had, which is "you're not my mother."

I am headed out to court this morning pondering the first year I had without her being a responsibility. Oh how I have needed this, and oh how I am so clear that if I did not have all the help I have right now, meaning her already being placed in a facility and doing well, I would not even consider this. I also had considered the other set of feelings, I wanted my daughter to be back with me being my family. We were starting to get close again since her initial intake. I was bringing my yoga mats for us as we were doing some together that I was teaching her. We would play soft music, pull up our mats and when I was done I would massage her back and hands. It was sweet for us. It was the closest we had gotten since she had been hospitalized. I had made a video of us with her smiling and saying sweet things and (kind of sassy like she was) saying to me

"Yes, this is my mother" as I was being my sassy self and saying something like "Lara's back with the person who's not her mother" or whatever I said. We both giggled together. I couldn't believe I had gotten to that point with her. It was such a breakthrough. I was so happy and content looking in her eyes.

The last day of that week, having packed up, I had in passing said something about her baby and how she did indeed have a whole new life waiting for her. She suddenly looked at me as if I were the Devil, as I saw the circles in the middle of her eyes transform from one dimension to another. Oh these eyes of ours that settle in a circular shape portray the same dimensions of the Universe. Looking in her eyes while she switched dimensions and watching the colors fade and the pupils get bigger was like watching a ship in outer space take off from one place and land in another. From one star in the galaxy tracing it to another constellation, from one cell in the brain wired to another tracing it together in a thought. The macrocosm of the stars, the microcosm the inner brain. I kissed Taylor goodbye.

Today Lara or Taylor rather, stormed in the courtroom late and threw herself down next to me where I was sitting in front of the judge, preparing for the hearing. With a charge of a bull, she said, "I don't know this woman," The judge looked at me when I was trying to interrupt her rule and said to me looking in my eyes: "Did you hear what she said. She doesn't know you." I was denied conservatorship over my own child.

I was vibrantly upset that the public guardian did not recommend me as well. He wrote down something about my medical marijuana use that I will further elaborate on that was expressed in a delicate setting, which also alarmed the judge. She indicated Lara did not need to be around that, as if I myself would subject her to anything after what I have been through. I tried to interrupt and explain but was quite shoved aside. The feelings of the Archons came rushing through my veins. I felt the terror then as if their blood was igniting through my pain and swimming their way around my defeat taking its breath knowing they really had my daughter. It was taking its breath over my separation from her. In an instant I was reliving being told to silence myself in the courtroom like I eventually was to have to in my grandson's court proceedings that were to take place.

What was not mentioned in the court was two or three weeks ago Lara did ask that I become her conservator. She had actually used my phone to call him. This was the week I was her mother, or at least she was fading out of the illusion. I felt so betrayed by the public guardian. All they did was see me work my ass off to help my daughter to have him not recommend me be her conservator. The Archons' job is to beat us at every area and every corner of our thoughts. I guess my personal Archon wanted this Cannabis issue to be brought forward so I could see that I really did believe in what I was saying about it and I stood by my words in the face of the courts and everyone. Nonetheless I was rejected; nonetheless I stood by myself and my belief systems.

My ego was affected badly. It has been extreme work for me to distance myself from the situation and detach from it where I would not take it personally. I believed at that time it would have been best for me to have Lara with me but the Archon or Taylor and or the beings that run Taylor have different plans for her.

The people that continue to run Lara, she continues to call "them," the "them" that keeps Lara at bay from her family is known to her as "The Law." Just as a side note here I want to tap you into some decoding of words that these darker forces do with us. One is they takes letters and flip them, hence the "M" would be a "W" or vice versa and they often read or write words backward. Hence "At Law," if we were to take the last letter and flip it equals the letter M, if you put those words together reading backwards this would be "MALTA." The Knights of Malta are the Jesuits that run our planet. Lara calls them" The Law!"

I will stand by my mothering and I will tell you no one has intuition like a mother to a child, it is wired in our DNA. I screamed at Brian B. her public guardian at the time, for not understanding the complexity of this and my side of this and how he handled it. He has not seen the work I have done with her nor has he been here for the whole story and I highly disagree with his choice due to the fact that Lara was starting to break through her psychosis. She had told me she associated me not being her conservator with me not being her mom. That is how her mind worked. I wanted her to dearly acknowledge me and break the psychosis.

Everyone has their way of coping and dealing with the hardest things thrown their way, some of those ways are super healthy and some are not quite pretty. This is what I did and it is quite well known later among the people at DCSF. I hold not one piece of emotion back, I don't think I should. I call and leave several messages. I leave screaming gut wrenching messages how we have all lost our way and how dare their stupidity add harm to my world, and that if they would recognize we were all one none of this bullshit would be happening. I call back again and make sure they got that message and then I call again and again until their voice box is full and that is the only message they receive that day is "We are all one."

Now I don't recommend this for proper manners and I certainly add in my insanity and my rage, but the intention is pure and I always had felt better. Sometimes I might have felt better at their expense though. I was not nice. I attacked at every angle even commenting on their physical appearance or anything I could do to hit them psychologically like they did me. I had to forgive myself for acting that way. I had often chanted everyday that their hearts would be protected from my rage but that I would be heard. I did not want to do damage to someone's heart, but that was the problem, their heart was not visible to me. Especially at DCFS, as I was later to encounter, they were machines to me, taking orders from the Illuminati and the dark leaders of our planet. That is a fact; that is not my anger talking as we have discovered history itself has been raped; it's all run under one dark unit. People are aware of this though and certainly not everyone agrees. I still keep them all in my prayers.

I wanted the psychosis, the DID (Disassociation Identity Disorder) concerning me not being her mother gone, as if I had control of it all. Later I recognized again that it didn't matter what particular illusion I was trying to break or not each time, she was still taken over. Drugs alone can take one over. Many addicts have Archons on them, as I further explain in the Archon Chapter. Nonetheless she is taken over. The Archons intertwined themselves between Lara and Taylor as the DID ignites.

Taylor had mentioned, "them" all had orders for her and her tribe from Mars to leave here. This is where my suspicions of Taylor being a Archon from another alien race inhabiting Lara's body (which I fully elaborated on in the Archon and M.K. Ultra chapters next,) increasingly grew. She talked about this in passing. She said that this was no longer a place they could inhabit. This I understood also to be where the Mars races will be reunited with earth, and vice versa. Again, as in truth, this is real. I touch on this elsewhere, On the other angle of it, the Alien Grays and Dragos are from the Orion Constellation; this is intertwined. They eventually set up shop on Mars. Taylor the Archon, whether a friendly invader or not was an invader and was giving me this information and Lara the person was nowhere in sight to keep Taylor in check, if there was going to be a transport and the aliens wanted Taylor's body housed by Lara.

As much as I have learned from Taylor, I am continuing to be deeply affected by her as she continues to operate Lara. It is my duty before my Creator to take care of me. I had at one point during all the court proceedings come to the idea that it was no longer healthy for me to be around my daughter until she herself could recognize me as her mother, until she herself decides I am her mother. Although, she herself is not there. Her being has stepped aside. She is my daughter, but she is not my daughter. She is not the entity I knew. I've started to have the feelings of having to beg someone to love me, and it just doesn't feel right. I start to think of that, and I think it really doesn't feel right especially because she **is** my daughter. I am her mother, and I need to be treated with respect whether she is sick or not. But am I her mother? There is another being inside her that says she has a mother. **Am I taking away a being from their mother now, I wonder?**

Even if my daughter is incapable of treating me the way I need to be treated, it is still not acceptable for me. It's no longer okay for me to take abuse from her whether she means it or not. It felt abusive to be constantly slammed in the face with her repeated attempts to remind me in the Archons' vibrant way that I wasn't her mother, especially after all I did for her. It's unacceptable whether the Archon is there or not, and if the Archon thinks it's going to get away with it, its job increases.

I am going to explain to you below in the Archon chapter that its job increases until you understand you are a Godlike Being, because it will challenge you until you become one, then when you become one with the all, the Supreme, it, the Archon, works as your personal serpent rather than the serpent working you. Satan or the advisory always said we need to judge him at the end of times. Did God assign the Advisory and or the Archons and the forms thereafter to unravel our subconscious beliefs that we are somehow separate from the source? It's important to understand this theory. It will render us much control. The Gnostics further speak of this.

I need to make sure I am giving myself the respect my daughter can't, even if my daughter is someone else. Although, because she is incapable, I am much more open to have compassion for her illness rather than anger. If she were capable of being in reality she would be. She would be with her son and her loved ones if she could be; that's all she ever wanted was a baby and a family.

I know, my higher soul, the Angel self, the self that is extraterrestrial, in tune with Source, can be looking at all this exactly in its ultimate truth at any given moment I need. My prayer the day prior to court was that if this decision or move for me to conserve my daughter meant in any way that I was to be harmed, that it would in any way hurt my daughter, or prevented me from expressing my highest good in life, then please do something to intervene.

The night before the yoga facility had asked me if I could sub the next morning, the same time court was. I was very torn because the last court hearing prior to this she chose to not show up for that first attempt to be conserved by me; where I was told that at the next hearing that I did not need to show up whether or not she were to come, it would be signed over to me, if all went well. (All had not gone well).

I tossed for hours before I had given the studio an answer of telling her I had had a prior commitment the next morning. She said, "No worries." They already had a sub teacher. I showed up in court the next day deciding in case there was a problem, I would be there, so I thought. Me showing up triggered my daughter even more I believe as she stormed in and sat down with anger next to me in court and made her continued stance that I wasn't her mother. I still kept trying to explain to the judge, in fact. I stopped her reading the verdict three times and interrupted her. It didn't matter, whatever it was. It is what it is now and I have to accept this.

I asked for the intervention if needed and it happened. I made a deal with Mother Father God about where I was in life and what I needed to do with me, myself, and "I" before court. I expressed that I would be 100 percent willing to take direction from the Mother Love of the Universe as I felt I was directed. That if I was to not focus on this situation with Lara then that was a direct sign that I was to continue my mission full force explaining to people the messages I have been getting from the Light Beings about the changes on our planet and the connections to the HIGHER DIMENTIONAL EARTH LIFE they show me. I knew this was creeping up on me, I was DIRECTED to write a MULTI -DIMENSIONAL ET BOOK explaining to everyone messages the higher beings tell us all on how they live life in the higher realms where all beings and civilizations abide by the LAW OF ONE. I have synonymously been working on this book as well as writing this. They seem to have fed each other well. I have had much conversing with the galactic and Ascended Masters throughout this book, which has put me in dictation mode, which leads me to the tablet as directed from the Light Beings.

CHAPTER 10
THE ARCHONS IN DETAIL
*WALK INS *VRILS *DJINNS

I was forced to learn about the dark. I continued to learn about the dark through the light. Every step of the way the Light Beings were educating me. Even I myself thought they were crazy and leading me into things that were mind-boggling for me, although it didn't matter, they just kept guiding and teaching me. We have been taught anything but the truth about other realms and other dimensions and what is in them. Sadly the truth has been taken and or the truth has been hidden. The other realms of our existence are something that is very well right here within our atmosphere. There is another entity and or energy being mimicked by technology or not that operates within my daughter's realms of her being, possibly your child as well, and perhaps others you know that you know or have a feeling that this is more than just addiction or mental illness. These energies and later entities we have come to be known as the "Archons." The Archons and their reality and our lack of education about them are in fact one of the main reasons I wanted to write this book. They are not demons attached to a body as we used to learn in The Exorcist. Think of it as bad energy run amuck. We as a society have been oblivious to these Archons, and all their DIFFERENT forms. It is important to go into a bit of history and length here about this as this has been one of the most misunderstood topics. We don't talk about this because the elites and darker forces have done a very good job at keeping themselves hidden, and we as the people have done a real good job cosigning most of their bullshit.

A Light Worker named Skye

I was cursed and blessed with starting to understand the "STDs," sexually transmitted deities. A woman named "Makalesi" under her YouTube page, describes these deities and the dark dominant energy that is repeatedly allowed to enter into one's own personal space during sexual transmissions. I also wanted to introduce Eve Lorgen, although you may have heard of her if you have been researching in this area. I go further into her work in the MK Ultra section. In her years of research and dealing with an array of people much like my daughter, and psychic vampirism, she talks about the same violations from the Archons and the Elites intermingled with them, or darker Alien races and fashions thereafter including our Shadow Government, taking over one's body and basically controlling minds and lives to various serious degrees. She even talks about the alien abductions that control one's love life. Many times they do this to get certain people together for various reasons benefiting them.

More and more I started to understand these things, things that were way different than the understandings of life I had when I grew up. STDs are not the only way an Archon will enter and captivate a person, the topic in and of itself is vast, therefore giving it a label of the "Archon Network." Abuse is definitely one way. I sickly thought of the rest of the women around the planet that have been abused or been in abusive situations, and how this made them all vulnerable. I was sickened this was the unknown therefore rendering us vulnerable. Many times when there is abuse there will be an Archon form, which is the actual "form!"

The Archons are real. They are entities that reside basically in the fourth dimension. The fourth dimension is understood to be the dimension of "The Collective." It is the dimension we must confront. The darker forces or beings that basically run this planet are masters at manipulating the hologram, the hologram we live in, consisting of multi- dimensions, dimensions where they exist. The Archons come in many forms and we must be aware of this. They are not just demon like souls with horns, (that is old school) rather demon like energies taking on many forms. They take on forms through other things such as your computer. Many Light Workers have computer hijackings from the Archons that will literally get in the way of your connections to the light. They also interfere with your personal plans and know everything about your deepest darkest fears and sit waiting for the igniting of them, for this is literally how they take their breath. On a larger scale many of the mass murders that are going on in the world have the Archons in charge of the master plan. It is important for us to understand it is not the person inside that body that commits a crime it is the Archon(s). Or in major cases such as school class room shootings or 911 where the elites intertwined with the Archon Network, hence the controller, manipulating one's perceptions, even about our planet.

We must also understand as a society that mental illness is one profound place you will find the Archons. I mention "Stewart Swerdlow," and there are so many others who will also explain this to you step by step in their work. The interest is this, "Which came first the mental illness or the Archon?" I will tell you in far greater cases than we are aware of, mental illness is a direct result of having an Archon inside one's auric field, and in most cases being controlled by a controller.

The Archons are indeed mentioned throughout history and have been also explained in the Gnostic and Hermetic teachings. The Koran is one of the best books on the Archons I have been told, as the Muslims are very privy to this information going deep into the Djinns. The "Gnostics" were eliminated by the church for exposing the Archons. There are many levels that exist within their order. Their mission is to prevent us from evolving and /or causing chaos. The reason for the chaos is so one can overcome profound obstacles, the obstacles that are in essence keeping one from being the "God Self" that one is. The obstacles also are understood what the Christians would label as the "SEVEN DEADLY SINS" contributing to the "FALL FROM GRACE," or where we as individuals have separated from Heaven ourselves and/or our heavenly selves. Once the obstacles are overcome, through extreme trials and tribulations, these "Archons" actually and amazingly enough will end up working for us rather than against us. They in essence become our serpents! Everyone's Archons may be different.

In Gnostic teachings, Makalesi explains the Creator God of this planet called the "Demiurge" has Archons controlling this evolutionary planet. If we go back to the Nuetru (below the Dark Lords), the AmiLord, and the AmiQueen, we see that one must pass these dark terrestrials in order to get out of the firmament that Planet Earth is under. Makalesi also describes the above in a bit more detail on her site. The Nuetru or the highest nature spirit beings, who where the higher Angels given the orders to create the evolutionary planet(s) here, created everything starting in layers. All of this correlates with the macrocosm of the planets down to the microcosm of our own personal Vortex Systems, hence our Seven Chakra Systems.

The main Seven are listed in categories as such that will correlate with the symbolic similarities between the Seven Planets, as well will correlate with the Seven Chakras of the body. The first is the Root Chakra focusing on the matters of the Physical, located at our perineum. The Root Chakra holds the color of red and is associated with Saturn. As such, the second is the sexual center right below the naval, associated with the color orange. The third is our Emotional Chakra located in the naval area. This area tends to greatly tighten when we are dealing with intense emotions, and its color is yellow. The fourth is associated with the matters of the heart associated with the color green. The fifth, our throat area deals with creative endeavors, communication, carrying the color of blue. The third eye of course is our intuition being the sixth, being of indigo color. The seventh, the Crown Chakra, deals with our connection to our higher realms and the Universe as a whole carrying the color violet. The Seven Deadly Sins will also correlate with each Chakra. When one Chakra center is kicked off balance, the seven deadly sins, hence the Archons, have an opportunity to take over. So much so an Archon has the ability to dominate that particular vortex center within the body. For example if the second Sexual Chakra is off balance, it will be based in lust, allowing a Archon to take over creating lustful crimes against our true nature of love. If the fourth Chakra is out of balance, the energy will be based in hatred rather than in love, allowing a lower Archon based in fear and hatred to dominate the person. When all these Chakra's and or planets (the microcosm) are out of alignment, we became separate from our ONENESS hence the fall from grace.

I felt the dark energy surrounding my daughter that horrific morning as the decent of her mind took place and the Archon entered. I felt the darkness, the emptiness, the horror and the beaming through as if a black goo-type energy was sucking the soul out of her. Miles Johnston talks about the black goo! I love his interviews. It was awful, so awful I don't think I was ever able to confront it until years later. I never looked at that because it was too dark, just to dark. Now although that I see and understand the light, I am not afraid of understanding the dark.

When I had met the higher beings, I was told that my darker experiences with the Archons were going to be of service to humanity. I continue to the flash back to the Alien Nurses that took me to complete my missions on this time line. Experientially I was to learn about the Archons. I have also had understandings of my multidimensional self once being from the "Orion Council of Light" through meeting with other high-profiled contactee that also confirm this during one of my private profound clearing sessions. Being from the "Orion Council of Light," it has been shown to me that one of my missions was to reincarnate and introduce or remind us of how to combat these darker forcers while incarnating on this planet. It is also what is dealt with being from the Melchizedic order. The order is an order the Light Beings have, I would say, come to us with!

Here is a list of how various religions or teachings in part relate to Archons. You, of course, can skip this part if you are not wanting more occult knowledge or detail, although I found it interesting.

Makalesi continues; In Gnosticism under the "Demiurge" or the Gods or "the Planets" are as follows: YALDABATH=SATURN, hence SATAN behind the Demiurge who created "ABARAX," which is controlling the 365 Archons or days, continuing on into the planets, IAO=JUPITAR, SABAOTH=MARS (Tuesday), ASTAPHANOUS=VENUS (love), ADONAIOUS=SUN (oneness), ELAIAOUS=MERCURY, HORAIOUS=MOON (aggression). Each has meaning. If they have a meaning in the astral, they have a tangible meaning in the physical.

Continuing in Gnosticism there is "SOPHIA" MOTHER OF ALL, the goddess deity, the Isis, Mary Magdalene energy, the divine female energy that has been left within us all. The energy is needed for one's protection from the Archons. ABARAX, who controls 365 Archons or days took astrology and perverted it. Meaning, linking astrology or, the current planets to misinterpretations of planets being pieces of rocks or the perverted version rather than the truth that these planets are real live beings: "PLANETS OF CONSCIOUSNESS." When we don't look at them and what they represent as real, they control us. When our own Kundalini (life force energy) is not activated, we do not look at them as consciousness, therefore these planets then do not become activated and we see them as dead rocks, which surpasses our senses and hence they become Archons or planets that govern, rather than serve. If our personal bodies do not have what I have mentioned, being the "Kundalini rising" or spiritual recognition of our being, we as well will turn to rocks hence allowing the Archons to take over our consciousness until we are forced to wake up and realize our "God Selves."

The Archons are also mentioned in the "Nagmahati" (NAG-MAHDI), a collection of fifty books found in the desert of Egypt in 1945, included in it are the Gnostic teachings and the teaching of the lost gospels of "Mary Magdalene." In the remaining forty-five books they talk about the Archons, the lower interdimensional beings that want to keep us in this type of prison or quarantine and have power over this realm, that work with our minds in a parasitic ways. This, I call accurate!

In Hermeticism they are also listed as follows (in general and not in order). SATURN=CALCINATION (ego, color red, this is also our first Root Chakra). JUPITER=DISSOLUTION (water, consciousness, subconscious, color blue). MERCURY=SEPARATION (observation, in its highest form it dismisses harm). VENUS=CONJUNCTION (green, Heart Chakra).

SUN=FERMENTATION OSIRIS (born again, color white).

MARS=DISTILLATION (Tuesday, transformation, coagulation).

MOON=MASTER KEY!

Likewise we see that the Angels in Christianity are listed as follows under their planetary signs; Angel Gabriel-Monday-Moon. Angel Sammeal—Tuesday-Mars. Angel Raphael—Wednesday-Mercury. Angel Sachiel—Thursday-Jupiter. Angel Aneal—Venus-Friday. Angel Cassiel—Saturday-Saturn. Finally, Angel Michael—Sun-Sunday.

A fellow Light Worker listed under the "13signsAstrology" YouTube page, talks about a deity pronounced aw-gone. "Ageawn" in the Vedic culture" is a fire deity, also known as "Agni." He is the fire deity that is responsible for slaying demons but friendly to humans. He actually is a deity that destroys the Archons. Renenutet, who is one of my favorites, pronounced ray-nu-net, the Goddess deity of the plants, is the deity that we can connect to when combating the Archons. We can ask and work with her. She is the wife of Re the Sun God. Since everything started out in darkness, as he explains, the "darkness is the supreme or where the true power lies", in essences- out of the darkness the elements were created. Therefore in all things there will be the darkness first. The darkness/ancient ones or Archons don't need life to live. It is a primitive force that is ramped and can take control if not nurtured properly through the deities or Sun, Air, Earth, Water, or if not nurtured properly through our own personal light. This primitive force running rampant takes over in darkness, manifesting in many different forms by taking over our minds since it is inherit in us.

We have to exist in the energy of the High Ancestors rather than the dark Archons. Renenutet, the Goddess of the plants is able to take this rampant energy and work with it using the energy and consuming it through her plants. Plants are Archons transmutation if you will, birthed to bring balance to the energy on this planet that the Archons were responsible for braking.

She knows the secrets to mastering the Archons is eating the particular creation that was birthed from these particular Archons. Similar to devouring our own demons created by ourselves. (Plant life brings balance. Algae seaweed, in the water governed by Renenutet came before or started before the Sun. Algae, seaweed energy before the Archons, energy grown from the Archons, therefore consuming plants transforms them). Renenutet is really the God of Archons. They don't want you to know this. In working with this Goddess to begin with, you must be a vegetarian from the beginning. She will not work with you unless you are because she deals with the earth. The earth elements are "structure." Taking control of your mind, she enables and wants you to work with the mind, overcoming temperas ways, she helps teach us how to use the magic plant-based elements to heal the Archons in the body, work with her. He says to chant with her, talk to her, ritual with her, raise a planet, and work with the earth element.

Interesting when I did more research on her she is also listed as the "god of protecting children."

Since in truth we are not restricted to linear time as our five senses understand them, we are in essence living all realities at once. Hence, the eternal moment of now. In this moment we are divided individualized expressions of the Divine. Depending on where you are on the evolutionary timeline or what dimension you are experiencing, you could be expressing a grand version of yourself or a lower version of yourself. The grand version, hence your Angelic Self or your Extraterrestrial self, the self that is ultrasensitive and able to connect to the higher realms within, therefore capable of creating an extra terrestrial outer world hence being able to see and you notice the Angelical realm and all her glories. Or, the lower version of yourself hence your devilish self will also express and experience itself depending on what degree you have fed it throughout your Over-soul's existence. That experience of the soul will incarnate into a form of darkness expressing itself in whatever demonic or Archonic way its fed. Many times we are literally facing Archons we ourselves have created, therefore this personal demon knows the darkest corners of our mind, therefore it is a master at being our own personal demon. Therefore the only way to really conquer that demon is to release it from its origin, hence within you.

The negative energy that they suck out of humans is called "fear;" fear is how these leeches stay alive. The one good thing about leeches is they do not last long. They are expendable through healing, but they are real. These leeches are just as real as Angels and orbs. We can't ignore this and it is wise to be aware of all the realms of our existence. Whether you can see yet or not it is important to gather knowledge, gnosis. Ignorance to this stuff is not knowledge or helpful and will render one powerless, especially in the case of a parent trying to protect their child.

I have sat with my daughter privately outdoors under the sunlight staring at her in the depths of her soul as she tells me that she feels very sorry for me that I cannot find my daughter. She tells me that the "Ward" took Lara and she is running around somewhere "out there in space." She talks about Lara being a mess and how she hurt everyone, how she is running around somewhere "out there in space," trying to find help but that she had done a lot of things. As I state she refers to the ward as "THEM." In one of the court proceedings concerning her guardianship, she had told the judge "THEM" was in charge of her life. She has often said "the Ward," hence "them" are the people running the planet. I translate this as, hence the shadow government, the shadow government and or versions of it that are in control of far more than just America.

The dark-shadow government, merging with the darker forces, (basically the ones that are in control of our Mental Health/Health Care Systems and all its aspects), are also greatly immersed in mind control, as you will understand, and have (seemingly) even far greater control than one ever could imagine. Control over one's electromagnetic energy field around their own body, using such things known as "Black Medi" technology, of whom a super soldier/whistleblower named Michael Ralph informed us. I in my own words just call it the **soul sucker** technology. I talk further of this below in the MK Ultra section. We have been robbed in many more ways than we can imagine. As in Lara's case and so many others using drugs where the energy around her body lowers greatly through the use crystal meth, allowing an archon to attach or lower energy forms that allow her aura to be open which allows the electromagnetic energy around her body to be controlled by a controller. Or Archon Network in general. Eva Lorgen speaks of Black Medi technology in a wonderful interview with Alfred Lambermount Weber. It's an incredible interview as far as getting information.

In my searching for answers, I have been to so many seminars around our country and have met several UFO experts. I mentioned Laura Eisenhower. President Eisenhower's great-granddaughter. I appreciate her work more than I could possible say. She is spot on relating to so much of what I mention here in my book with my personal experiences. I did not think that this could ever be explained but I learned people like her had already had a dead-on handle on this stuff. I was floored with happiness. I could not believe someone really understood the Archons and how our Government really does have an involvement with this issue that has trickled all the way down to affecting my child and so many others that have been cast as mentally ill or insubordinate in some manner. She gives a detailed reading of how these Archons relate to your personal life, as she gives personal sessions on how to work with them.

I tell you, as you were somehow drawn to my book, I am not the only mother experiencing this. I am not the only parent that has sat there and literally watched their once sweet adorable loving child become another entity or out and out watched them being controlled. There are several parents that are so desperately lost not understanding where their child went. Literally, I am not the only mother/parent that has said there is another being inside of my child that she **is** hearing. **IT IS NOT JUST MENTAL ILLNESS** here!

You are not crazy and neither is your child. These energies are real. These serpent energies of the Archon order are real and they are dominating people, especially people that do not have inner strength, or who are reliant on something outside of themselves for their good and their brilliance. Such as addicts. When one goes outside of themselves for anything other than the divinity within, the Archons are masters in taking over when able. Their energies are low enough for them to dominate one's being whose Chakra's centers are open. Eva Lorgen, author of Love Bites also mentions this in her brilliant interview under "Ep9 Eva Lorgen, The Alien Agenda." It is an interview worth listening to, in fact all her work is.

A Light Worker named Skye

"John Lash," another well-known researcher on the occults and the Archons, states, "The Archons are those who invade our minds. The Archons access our human thoughts telepathically stimulating the mind, they affect our imagination and use the power of make believe."

Taylor's mannerisms are much different than Lara's. Taylor is much more cooperative or mundane I should say. "I am sorry ma'am, I am not your daughter," she would say. She doesn't react to much not even later watching all this stuff that was to later alarmingly unfold in court with her son. Even when Taylor gave birth, she was almost numb, I think she uttered a word "ouch" one time. While I was in labor for her I screamed like I was being murdered and it lasted thirty-three hours, ironically enough.

"The Invisibles" he calls them, mentioned in Cobra's interview with Alexandra Meadors, March 2014—"Cobra" is well known in the underground world for being a well-formed whistle blower. You may know of him and his work. His information is quite accurate in many ways. Some will argue he is informed so much that he is an informant himself or part of the Controlled Opposition rink, such as Alex Jones. Either way you will always get truths from people that are working with both. It is part of the occult practice, as I state, to always let the oppositions know of its moves in plain sight. It is not for me to decide on people and who they are, rather what bits of information are sent our way that rings true with what is real.

What is well known and what is real and going on in our world is how our darker government directly is affecting not just Targeted Individuals, T, I's, and politicians but our kids and our youth are under attack from the Archon Network with advance technology from Alien races. I love the interview. It is quite accurate in the information I get on the Archon Network and Electromagnetic Energy. He just calls them "The Invisibles". He relates to it as such. In general he talks about them being entities and energies (that I elaborate on further in the MK Ultra chapter) that are part of the anomaly that have infested the thinking process. The thinking process's which has been diluted by the hologram. Entities and energies which are part of the illusion process that went wrong in a certain phase after the creation of the light, in this galaxy. Very similar to the Gnostic teachings as well as what John Lash and Laura Magdalene Eisenhower talk about when explaining the origins and the cosmic burst, if you will. The thinking process that has been hijacked!

52

*WALK INS

I have also been made aware of the beings in other realms that do what is called a "WALK IN" and take over a body by their soul walking into another person's body. It is an agreement that takes place between both souls. Usually the "Walk Ins" are in the room observing the soul that is about to exit the body. This is usually done when there is a life path where the soul is having a difficult time such as an accident or an illness or a major break in someone's life.

There are not only Walk Ins of the lower self, there are also Walk Ins of a grand kind, that many Light Workers can even relate to. The difference is the light Walk In will announces itself and what it is doing. The dark will not. The light Walk In will also sometimes fluctuate between personalities, such as the Tibetans talk about when one goes into a psychosis. All Walk Ins happen or enter the body when there is a major break in someone's life such as in the case with my daughter. Although let me stop and interfere as it was given to me. I talk an awful lot of my daughter's tragedies but I was reminded, again, of mine, by the Light Beings.

I myself was at the supreme breaking point in my life when I met the Light Beings. I was requesting to be taken off planet. I laid on the floor for three days in sweat, trembling, not being able to reach my soul. I returned with heightened states of understandings and a vibrancy for life. I suddenly understood the light and its directions. And most of all I knew without a doubt I was One with all creation. That all was not there before the death of my lower self, or before I laid there in front of my Altar. I walked into my life in a new way from then on. It has never stopped. The Kundalini expression in me will not let it. I am out of the Matrix. Although still in human form having human experiences, I have been told more than once I personally have been a Walk In in my higher form. Perhaps on some level my daughter and I are really twin souls expressing both light and dark. I always wondered if in my last incarnation I was on the dark side and she was on the light. To me personally it is an upgrade of DNA, a call sent out from our Creator to many now.

In the Emerald tablets of Thoth it speaks about there being interdimensional types of reptilian beings that were able to subduct those that sit on the throne today and have connected to the blood line of the elites of the world.

A Light Worker named SKYE

Emerald tablet number VIII
Far in the past before Atlantis existed,
men there were who delved into darkness,
using dark magic, calling up beings
from the great deep below us.
Forth came they into this cycle.
Formless were they of another vibration,
existing unseen by the children of earth-men.
Only through blood could they have formed being.
Only through man could they live in the world.

In ages past were they conquered by Masters,
driven below to the place whence they came.
But some there were who remained,
hidden in spaces and planes unknown to man.
Lived they in Atlantis as shadows,
but at times they appeared among men.
Aye, when the blood was offered,
for they came they to dwell among men.

In the form of man they amongst us,
but only to sight were they as are men.
Serpent-headed when the glamour was lifted
but appearing to man as men among men.
Crept they into the Councils,
taking forms that were like unto men.
Slaying by their arts
the chiefs of the kingdoms,
taking their form and ruling o'er man.
Only by magic could they be discovered.
Only by sound could their faces be seen.
Sought they from the Kingdom of shadows
to destroy man and rule in his place.

But, know ye, the Masters were mighty in magic,

able to lift the Veil from the face of the serpent,
able to send him back to his place.
Came they to man and taught him the secret,
the WORD that only a man can pronounce.
Swift then they lifted the Veil from the serpent
and cast him forth from the place among men.

Yet, beware, the serpent still liveth
in a place that is open at times to the world.
Unseen they walk among thee
in places where the rites have been said.
Again as time passes onward
shall they take the semblance of men.

It continues on to explain the descriptions of the reptilians that are controlling the planet.

I wanted to state something interesting about demons that was given to me by a demon himself. His name is ALFAARAA. You can look him up. He is able to go back and recall the demon life(s) he has lived throughout time and has found he had much to do with great separation on our planet. He is giving the planet a wealth of information about demons. I wrote him a note concerning my daughter and this is the response: *(I did not edit any of it for grammar reasons as this was irrelevant) Here he is continuing to explain to me how he sees these attachments:*

"Next Demons attach to humans to FEED we provide FOOD as emotional energy. Demons feed on Emotional energy aka Drama. All of us have the Demon? Demoness inside of Us this is the EGO/Mind. It is Actually a soul fragmented from the Earth consciousness that Rules over the Flesh. Its Purpose is to Create the Drama and Darkness, the Soul than Brings light to that Darkness in an Equal amount thus YOU have grown and are returned to Balance

-this is how it works...The Demon almost always will not allow anything else into its temple aka the body. So other Demons can and will

attach to the outside around the back of the neck area and the solar plexus area they from the outside feed off of the scraps left by the Internal Demon. What happens depending upon the number of Demons is there is NOT Enough food. Drama must be Increased the flesh body is a victim..

SHE has no control, well only AFTER tremendous drama when all the Demons are FED then SHE might possibly come through..However in some circumstances, "The Demon" controlling the Inside allows the Others or Another to Enter and Take control of the physical body.

UNDERSTAND THIS HAS NOTHING TO DO WITH HER SOUL; IN FACT THIS MAY FORCE A WALK IN AND THROW THEM ALL OUT.

I KNOW THAT DRUGS HAVE BEEN INVOLVED, DRUGS ATTRACT DEMONS THEY ALSO REDUCE DEMONS AS THE DEMON INSIDE IS REDUCED IN POWER WHILE THE BODY IS DRUGGED SO TO SPEAK, THIS IS WHEN IT COULD HAVE HAPPENED.

ALLFAARAA

I recall one time Lara called screaming at me to come down to her apartment, "Mom you don't understand, come down, stay here, get over here!" she kept screaming. I couldn't handle the way she was demanding this of me so I went nowhere. She said someone was shooting her and I said call the cops. She did and of course there was no one there shooting her as the cops swarmed in with their guns, although in her mind she was terrorized. I too was terrorized knowing she was terrorized, later when I knew what I knew. I was appalled how much these guys really do have their minds taken over.

I always thought I related to everything, and actually I do to a huge level. I understood what it was like to connect with other beings that were not understood by others and I also understood other realms so to me conversations of an ET Angelic source are normal. As within bipolar or a delusional schizophrenic mind, the dopamine levels are raised to a point where it reaches the euphoric centers resembling the connection to the third eye that is connected to the DMT centers within us. This is the code, which is the code of our Oneness, which has the same universal information in all of creation. I had tapped into this information when I had my Kundalini rising or third eye awakening. I understood all this, but the one thing I could not understand was what it was like to actually have a voice in your head that was in seemingly command of your physical actions and what you saw and heard.

It fascinated me to sit down and talk to the people who have experienced this once the mind control stops. They will tell you there is a voice that is directing them and it is not theirs. They in turn are so misunderstood that the average person just treats them as if they are "crazy" and the person talking to them feels that whatever they are trying to say, do, or feel is being disregarded. Sadly then there is no in inside their mind. On top of that the person who **really is** connecting to other realms or "controller(s)", of course is alone and completely misunderstood and terrified of what is in their head to begin with, which just promotes more isolation from this reality and deepens into other realties. When they get the vibe that everyone is shutting them out, the instinct is to go within, and they go so far within it may be hard to get them out.

I recall having a conversation with a client of mine who took the time to talk to me about what it was really like to have your mind taken over when there is a voice that has more control than your own voice. The closest I had come was induced with an Ambien pill, Vicoden, and wine. That somewhat lethal cocktail had me in a hallucinatory state on one or two experiences where I slept, walked, talked, and saw others that weren't there. That's, of course, because I was induced with chemicals that twisted the wiring so bad that reality was far off, not because there was someone in there directing me that I was hearing. It somehow brought my attention to once my daughter seeing me in a trance like state vibrantly upset crying over her situation and how devastating it was for me, she had walked in on one of my crying sessions. To my amazement she kept saying "Whose got my mom"? Whose got my mom?" as if there really was someone to "get" me, to take over me. It was my clue throughout that there was indeed a "Controller" in her mind. I continue further in the MK Ultra chapter below

A Light Worker named SKYE

Many others I have spoken with through the years describe it as such. They are controlled by a voice in their head that directs their moves. About twenty years ago I also remember meeting a guy who was in AA, Alcoholics Anonymous. He had full blown "schizophrenia" so to speak, although I will tell you it was the Archon Network, induced by drugs. He had been treated and on medicine and was sober. He explained to me that the voices would always direct him. He would say he would be directed to walk barefoot to the west side of the river in Dayton, Ohio, and he would do whatever he was directed to do. That sounds like an experiment, that I further elaborate on in the MK Ultra Chapter.

My conversation with my client went the same exact way. He was taking dictation from a voice. When I looked back at the nights that Lara called me screaming that there was someone in the house shooting her or that there were voices everywhere I made her sit in it alone. I have very mixed feelings about that, which was how it became torturous for me. I was educated on mental illness. I understood that there were voices there, although I did not understand the depths of Electronic Harassment or Mind Control that took someone and how terrified they were. Lara was screaming in terror for me to come help her because of those voices. I would always try to teach her how to work with the voices as best I as could, although I later learned there are great people who could have helped her even more who have had first experience with this such as Solaris Blueraven, who I mention in the later MK ULTRA chapter. I knew, although, how to work with spirit voices because I knew the glory of spirit. When you have that, you have no fear and fear is what they operate off of. Lara was swimming in the lower dimensional vibrations of the Root Chakra, using drugs. There was no way she was not going to be controlled by it.

I had felt so sorry that her mind had to experience such horror. Oh God, it made me cringe at what she had to feel, although I also was equally bold about that. If she made the choices she did that continued to open portals to other realms then that was what she was going to get. It wasn't until later I really understood the complexity of when the Archon does actually take over. This does not render the situation powerless. It just brought more compassion.

Mental illness is such a complex situation because what doctors tend to forget is there are other realms that we are communicating with and there are other beings these people are listening to. Now we know the place in the ethereal where the voices are **is** being controlled as I continue to explain in MK ULTRA section. Most doctors want to dismiss this and medicate it as if that was the problem. This is not the problem. Listening to other spirits is not a problem, just like listening to other people is not a problem unless they are controlling you.

One can usually protect their Chakra or the vortex energy field by keeping their Chakra's or the energy fields around the body strong, but when there is a portal that is open for darker forms to enter it is quite difficult. There are so many illnesses due to having damage in one's Chakra field. There are so many distorted minds because one has their Chakra points open to darker situations. I wanted her to understand that if she chose drugs that this whole thing is also what she chose, but because her mind doesn't associate drugs with consequences there was little I could do. It tortured me not being able to help her, although the times that I did go to sit with her were hell for me.

I sat there in an apartment filled with dog feces, cockroaches, rats that smelled awful, spending a few nights here and there to help with the voices. Although my body's energy was so wiped from life, one night of sleep like that was physically and emotionally detrimental to my well being at the time. I could not do it. It was such a feeling of helplessness. I wanted to help her, but I also knew the only way I could possibly even almost help her was to not help her and make her find her own power that would ward off her own demons.

*VRILS

** This is separate from my daughter's issue but for the state of recognition I want to bring in one more subject you may have come across on your findings if you have been researching this. It has also been mentioned that people are also taken over in the physical as there is an actual race called Vrils (part of their Archon race) that are, physical creature beings, according to Donald, that they use to capture a human's soul through a very odd process that he explains will take out the human soul and insert the lizard's soul. It's a Luciferian thing. Again we were warned of this by the Essences and Gnostics, and I believe a few Apostles. Interestingly enough this practice is also known to be an ancient one, wondering if it was stemming from the mystery religions of ancient Babylon and Egypt. Exactly what I had mentioned in my letters to the courts again that the Gnostics warned us about.

If I may take a paragraph to elaborate also on ***Djinns**. When there is an Archon, it would be more difficult, because most people as of yet have no idea what that means. They automatically think like the movie The Exorcist. That's not true. That's demonic possession of a satanic takeover. Archons can range from more of the subtle alien or off dimensional ethereal invasion (that has already happened); the amoeba like energy around people and the planet. To the big time Archons known to incarnate into world leaders!) The **leech**, the **black goo,** are all energy patterns that can come in many forms from a character trait (even a smoking cigarette leech) to eventually an actual being, a Djinn or the Archon (Djinn are similar to Archons, same theme and they to shape shift). Mental illness is associated with the takeover of the soul, and or sucking off the original soul from the Archon or Djinn or Alien, as well as associated MK Ultra and electronic harassment.

Now that I have given you the history of the Archons in some detail, I am going to bring history back to how it all relates to humans in the here and now in our day-to-day lives and in the courtrooms we all go to. I would like to share with you portions of a very serious but dark letter(s) that was written to several judges here in Los Angeles County that I was to encounter later in the most difficult of situations. These letters will inform you of information as to where and how these beings play a role on our planet and in our government. (Some of these are graphic).

The following is a portion of the actual letter: This is the first of several letters, as I mention. These letters in general explain to us much of what is going on, as well as, continues on with my story with my daughter, as well as introduces the many deep serious topics we as humans are being faced with.

"After a series of tragic events in my life one being the illness of my daughter, I had a documented profound spiritual experience that allowed me to awaken with heightened sensitivities that ignited my Akashic Records connecting me to such things as telepathy, astral travel, and remote view. Remote view on our country and what is really going on in our planet. This profound spiritual experience has me in contact with what is known as a form of "Light Beings." They explain to me I am Light Worker genetically coded to

have portions of my memory returned to me at this time frame on our planet. These are interdimensional beings, extraterrestrial ET/Angelic beings of pure love. They have been in contact with hundreds of thousands of people like myself now with the same information, preparing us for the changes that are to take place here on earth (and within our government) for the return of our "Ascended Masters and our Galactic Family," which we as humans will all be interacting with. Although I am a Buddhist, much of this is explained in the Bible in Genesis, the Magaharhati, the Nag Mahati, and of course the Vedic's and Sumerian text. I did not quite know how to explain this until I ran across an interview with a man named Dr. Bob Dean, a US Army sergeant of NATO intelligence. His findings are very accurate as to what is happening to many humans like myself. He will also explain to you about the new Indigo Children being born that each of you must fully understand now. You may also understand we are at the end of times as we understand it and that the new Golden Age is approaching. In order for this to take place, there needs to be much clearing of the darker forces that you may know have been running our planet, and a plan is in place in vast proportions. Perhaps you are aware of this as well. In preparing for this, the Illuminati with the darker forces of the Kabal (Insertion; consisting of members of the Majestic 12) are following the biblical script in order for humanity to be misled and have prepared us for a NWO takeover by the darker races.

I am going to explain to you step by step how this is so very real and how you each are involved far greater than you may understand. As you will come to know, earth was taken over by the darker reptilian races (insertion: originally known to earth as the Astro Alba's) that have invaded earth during the Atlantean and Lumerian fall. We as humans found this out during World War II when Eisenhower was confronted by certain lower alien races, as the atomic bomb interfered with other atmospheres. There were several negotiates. We were asked to give up our nuclear weapons. We did not. We sent out a stress call and were met by other ET and alien (there is a difference) races as well. Some were benevolent, and some were not, both with advanced technologies. In a nutshell the presidents who were wanting to give humanity freedom and technologies and free energy to help the planet with our benevolent races were disposed of. Other presidents were actually humanoid reptilians themselves, far advanced beings of the Reptilian Satan race (insertion: and or service their dark lord known as their Omnipotent Hynes Krall). They believe they own this planet. They are advanced beings and are very capable and well known for being shape shifters into leadership and take human forms. They came from other planets in our solar system 26,000 years ago from the Orion star system and are part of the Drago and Reptilian system. They came from other planets in our solar system that needed to be cleared of their own evil and darker entities, forces, and ways. May you understand we are the last planet in the entire solar system to rid ourselves of the Darker Forces. They are responsible for all the major wars as they pin humanity against each other posing as terrorists. Rob Potter, a well-respected speaker in UFology explains the following set up to you quite well.

They did this by setting up chambers inside the earth for what is known as their "Implementation Process," setting up an artificial environment, an Eden. From there they utilize their superior mind control technologies. They understand the human condition very well. They are in control of what is called incarnation grids, which controls their bloodline and also presents us with a very false Matrix. They are able to Mind Control us in various superior ways, one, deliberately through our judicial system, as many of our judges are self appointed leaders from the darker races as equally and eloquently stated in ET 101. Also through Media, Microwave Radio Waves, Cellular Waves, Cellular Spider Waves in church towers, Fluorides, Vaccines, which calcify our pineal gland for the lowering of our dmt (dimethyltryptamine) levels, our "Third Eye of Spirituality." Another deliberate way mind control takes places is through what you must and will come to know (or already do) as Leeches and the hierarchy of that is through the Archons. Archons come in many forms and the hierarchy of that is Satan/ Abbarax and alive everywhere even in our electronics, there are levels of them and their strengths. Especially now since December 21, 2012, the quarantine is off Planet Earth.

They (a full blown Archon) are what was attached to the Sandy Hook situation, Archons aka "hidden controllers" working for the dark. Some Leeches are even genetically hybridized, created through our shadow gov-ernment and the darker Alien Gray Reptilian races residing in many of their underground bases.(Insert: even the Gray Reptilian beings themselves can be manufactured in these bases). They are manufactured for the sole pur-pose of being a soldier for the dark, making sure we continue to believe it *is humans that are evil terrorists against each other. There are also android soldiers without emotions so when the time is right we all take orders from the New World Order. There are actual interviews with them from our people at "Project Camelot." They use words like "it's not sentiment, depopulation, and we are not all equal." (Insertion: There are also Super Soldiers to combat the negative ones.) There are also the same reptilian races that are free floating dust particles that form amoeba like forms able to attach to the human aura. These are what I will explain is involved in many of your court proceedings as I believe I experienced this firsthand myself. All in a ploy to take over Mother Earth and make humanity believe that they are separate from each other, separate from Prime Creator, and convince us that we were not meant to be Godlike beings. We are, and our Godlike selves will eventually destroy them, then all the planets in our Galaxy can be restored to Prime Creator's original plan for us, which was the real Garden of Eden.*

**A trait of the Illuminati is they always give us eloquent clues in plain sight. Hence tracing every major building in DC, winding into a perfect pentagram facing down. The White House also faces the star system Sirius A, where the Orion Council sets. Another eloquent clue, is a US judge sitting at a rectangular desk with other square shapes around them in a black robe specifically resembling leadership of the darker races over the planet. This is explained in detail in many of Michael Tsarion's seminars as well as other scholarly individuals.

These reptilian leaders of our country (behind the scenes) and the participates in the Judicial System from the darker side have their superior underground bases all over the planet usually following grid lines and guarding our once holy star gates to other realms. There are some main ones now under New Berlin, with the Illuminati and their Controllers the Jesuits...

There is a bit more to that fourteen-page letter of what is really transpiring on our planet and how we are directly involved. I released other portions later on, as the events in our lives unfolded. I decided, although, to insert this portion for a clearer, basic understanding of the Archons. Later, I go into how there is a massive force happening on our planet far greater than we have ever or will ever see, to rid these beings of our planet. It's vast. It's grand, and it's happening. I will go into much detail about this too.

CHAPTER 11

MK ULTRA;

CLONES

As I have mentioned, one of the most blatant and vital parts of the whole Archon Network and how the dark Kabal operates with the War on Humanity, targeting our teenagers and young adults, is through, Mind Control, MK Ultra or Electronic Harassment, in one way or another. I will further break it and its origins all down in this section.

I am going to get right to the facts when it comes to this particular section. I also want to state before the following paragraphs that I never once believed my daughter just had mental illness. I did not believe this particularly because I was meant by the Light Beings that had me informed to understand what was going on our the planet.. So to me this in general was sounding like what the beings have been telling me. It wasn't until after directed investigation from them that I understood how it all took and/or takes place in the physical realm. One of the most frustrating things for me was, I knew, that others looked at my daughter as if she was an addict, or insubordinate, or had a "mental break," without the whole theme. She suffers from addiction or "mental illness" was what the doctors and friends and family digested.

That is all they knew. They were not educated in or on Mind Control, MK Ultra/Electronic Harassment or the Archon Network whatsoever. Even the well-intended people I knew who had their own periods of "voices" in their head did not understand the Archon Network and or Mind Control. They just can't in their mind comprehend this. We are conditioned erroneously as a society to have problem/solution based formulas. This is not the case. We are horribly wrapped up in believing problem=mental illness. Well okay that must mean medication and behavioral therapy=solution! Well what if the definition of the problem has been deliberately tainted. Although to me, not what if in any way shape or form, it has period, and the sooner we realize this as a society the quicker we will get those formula based solutions; **IS THIS REALLY MENTAL ILLNESS OR MIND CONTROL?**

This is something I find to be the most interesting part of it all. Her reality we call delusional is indeed an actual reality (as well). There is a world in the ethereal consisting of many ET and alien beings in other dimensions that has made itself real in our dimension and the mentally ill or ones labeled as mentally ill have a sensitivity to this. We have been taught through beliefs taken over by the shadow government that these people were crazy, when in fact, I later learned how un-crazy these people were. They were not crazy. They were in touch with the different parts of reality and different dimensions that are not visible to most. In fact, such things as schizophrenia occurs because the shadow government has a harder time dummying down these beings, dummying them down by keeping one stuck in our false Matrix. They are the biggest targets for Mind Control, because their mind is so powerful!

The schizophrenics, for one thing, will be the first to tell you about all the nonsense and demonic happenings going on over the television waves. They can't stand television and for a good reason. I learned so much and how even those seemingly meaningless statements of disliking television were not meaningless nor were they made to agitate me.

Mk Ultra is a very complex sophisticated program. One way the experiment originally was done, before modern advancement of the technology that came in to play, according to a former member from the CIA, is by administering drugs, LSD, and combining sensory deprivation (sleep, water, food, light). The drug in general allows the person to be under a form a mind control. The CIA experimented with this with our children in the seventies. CIA programmer researcher professor "Delgato" wrote in "Physical Control of the Mind" in 1969 that brain transmitters can remain in a person's brain for life. The energy to activate the brain transmitter is transmitted through energy frequencies. **The Reptoids/Kabal have access to this frequency**.

LSD can be very much like a neurotransmitter, theory stated, that something was wrong with these transmitters, what they then tried to do was create an artificial psychosis, a psychosis they are in control of. In other advances they also insert chips behind the subject's eye, as many survivors will now testify to. Both allow the person to see themselves as "THE CONTROLLER," "THE HANDLER."

Sex Slave, (beta programming) is a combination of (alpha programming) overall rewiring of one's neural mechanics a necessary precursor for any form of more specific programming.

Beta Primordial (primitive mind) for sex programming—this program eliminates learned moral convictions and stimulates the primitive part of the brain (the hind brain, aka reptilian brain) in order to perpetuate inhibition-less sexual instincts. This training program, usually for women, is developing the ultimate prostitute for a sex machine for their handlers and or programmers. The aim of the Illuminati programmer when making a beta Mind Control Subject (MCS) is to restrict (but not completely) the mental areas used by the sex slave to alter the hindbrain, making them an animal, hence more reptilian and also making them programmable at will. The controller/handler or the programmer can send suggestions to the victims through calculated hand movements or specific trigger words that are used to send one off into a programmed state without even realizing it. This is also done in modern time electronically through the handler and or an AI, "Artificial Intelligence," in general.

This is not just operating for sexual purposes on our youth; many of our high-powered politicians are targeted individuals or "TIs." Also I have mentioned celebrities and judges. These TIs are **interfaced** with the technology and/ or electronically mind controlled by either the AI the "Artificial Intelligence" running the planet or whatever handler they have. You can see the interference if you are privy to it. They use an Interface. Very much like a musician that uses an interface to transfer the electronic codes from the instrument through the interface to a computer allowing it to be decoded and transferred. The interference we see with mind control is done through the interface. A Controller or Handler has the interface. We here of the names who are using these interface technologies from such people as mentioned Cathy O'Brien. There are many coming forward now. I could see what I called the interference with Lara so very many times. We would be walking and she would just suddenly stop. Oh I hated seeing this. She would suddenly be stopped as if someone was talking to her and she was taking orders. It was as if she entered another reality. She did. She would answer them often replying and or just shaking her head saying, "Yeah, yeah, yeah…wait space." I can't tell you what seeing her like this did to me. I hated it. I wanted to, and do actually tell them, her voices, aka the handlers (in any way) to fuck off and what a joke they are compared to the Christ energy. Although it's her mind, she will be made to do that herself under our Creator. I am quite sure though I already have my dip in her handlers karma, there is no way in all of eternity this will not be brought to the light with me behind the scenes. I am a Light Worker for this planet. I will not return to my kingdom until this situation is cleared and I have understood that the handlers have reaped what they have sown

I was mortified at the truth as many around told it to be. It was matching my supreme consciousness, where the Light Beings lie. Mortified that we as a society keep ticking under this insane madness. Sad that MK Ultra is used on many of our celebrities. They are (they/their clones) are basically used as slaves to support satanic messages getting to our airwaves from the dark races. They make damn sure that the masses are fed things to the public. They subconsciously have people in one way or another literally under their spell, unless you have been taken out of the Matrix or have become aware yourself.

I mention Eve Lorgen. Of all the people I have researched I will say she has mentioned what has happened to my daughter in the most precise ways. Equally to Solaris I would say. She has reported endless accounts of people like my daughter and I highly suggest learning from her. I have explained to you how the Archons enter into one's auric field, but that is not the only way a soul is invaded. It is imperative we understand there is technology used to parasitize us just like the Archons do. In fact much we have learned **is** done through technology, as in not demons but induced, technology that allows one to have a parasite being attached to one's auric field. This parasite or interdimensional being can be a parasite in various forms such as a Grey, an Archon, another Alien race, a host, a temporary amoebalike form, etc., or whatever is needed. They (hence, the Controllers) use what has been known as Black Medi

A Light Worker named Skye

Technology, as I earlier mentioned I would explain. This was also discovered from a super soldier named Michael Ralph. The Black is for Black Magic; the Medi is for Medical. She talks about and confirms what I have known from the Light Beings. I just had no idea whatsoever that someone had it all explained.

Eve talks about how many of the mental facilities that patients are taken to are, in truth, owned by secret occult leaders or societies. This is intentional. The experiments that are currently being done on the mentally ill are ones that allow the individual to be controlled in the ethereal. They do not out and out torture the mentally patients like they did in the old days, so no worries there. They have rather upgraded their invasions through violently attacking one's spirit being. They don't need to come in and strap my daughter down to a gurney and stick needles in her eyes. They have done it to our children and mental patients pretty horrifically without even coming an inch near the person.

The invasion happens by using one's Chakra system through trans-dimensional technology. The trans-dimensional technology allows entities and parasites to come through this artificial porthole. Again we are electromagnetic beings. They mimic this energy around our bodies. The technology is also able to take out one's soul and replace it with one of an Alien being. This is way more common than you and I may have ever known. In whatever manner, my daughter's soul perhaps has been removed from her body, as I can see at this time frame. Taylor has entered. Taylor is controlled by another source. They (Lara and Taylor) both have mentioned there is a common "Communication System." As I often state, my daughter has mentioned celebrities on this communication system, each celebrity she has mentioned has been linked to the Illuminati or MK Ultra such as Michael Jackson, Tupac, and Britney. For years before Lara was hospitalized, she used to say over and over to me, "It is a communication system, mom, communication, it's communication." She later would state that whoever "had her," she would sometimes call him daddy or a weird slang name like Doo Doo, and that she would be in big trouble if she continued contact with us.

Eve also talks profoundly about how these beings can enter into one's auric field naturally through crystal meth. This is how I believe it all started with my daughter. This was much more common then I even knew. I knew it was possible, but I did not know how very common it was. The Archons as I

68

mention can do this naturally through one's porthole, through drugs or sexual energies. This procedure is being mimicked through technology. They are also aware they can do it in a strip clubs through others sexual juice energy that is transmitted there so to speak.

This Black Medi Technology is known to be used for various reasons and from various ET races. It is current; it is on earth. Eve talks about a strip club in a well-known place that has this technology that is used on their patrons. The bank next door that operates this technology is owned by the Illuminati. They target various individuals for various reasons. Much is found to be for experiments to electronically control the population.

I have to mention here as well how very grateful I truly am. Some of these TIs or targeted individuals are ritual abuse experience-ers that have been through some very serious stuff on the physical level. Lara got it all basically in the ethereal, affecting her mind. That was and is horrific. I felt deeply for all the others that had the physical ritual abuse. Many of these TIs have been kidnapped and raped since childhood and by family members. I nor my family was subject to satanic rituals or any such thing. I am familiar with so many stories being a Light Worker and I will not stop my work for these people because I am a Light Worker. It is very hard to hear what so many have gone through. I was equally powerfully proud that so many have really overcome this. I was proud of our human genetic coding. I knew the ones that have overcome this had ignited their genetic coding to the Supreme within them.

Solaris Raven, someone who I personally respect because of her accuracy, too, has a wonderful radio show, as do others in this field. She can spot the interference of one's mind as well. "It's interesting to hear and see others talk that are under mind control," she states. "Often times they are broken with their dialogue. You will also often times see them using hand signals," Solaris says, "according to what their handler wants." She describes George W. Bush and Reagan both in communication with **Interface Technology**. She could see him, referring to Bush, being compromised. Many are being compromised by nuerolinguistic programming.

Also one, a gifted medical intuitive, a very well known person in the research of Mind Control, who I mentioned earlier, Stewart Swerdlow, is a clairvoyant who has the ability to see auric fields and personal archetypes as well as read DNA sequences and mind-patterns. His great-uncle, Yakov Sverdlov, was the first president of the Soviet Union. His grandfather helped form the Communist Party in the United States in the 1930s. Swerdlow talks about how this is done particularly on our vulnerable young ones that are either mentally ill or subject to drug abuse. Particularly this is in reference to his interview with Solaris Ravin, "Freedom Slips Radio" (2-23-2014). There are archives anyone can order.

Cobra talks about the Archons as being parasites, which infest the etheric brain, the astral brain, and mental brain, therefore compromising the thinking process. The thinking process is a creation of sequences of thoughts that gets initialized by firing electromagnetic signals with neurons in the ethereal mental and astral brain. When interfered with by the parasite, the person cannot make clear thoughts. The wiring is interfered or compromised by parasitic beings. He describes them as beings from higher realms in our brains, indicating when infested one cannot make logical conclusions, much like the echoes of Mind Control! This Alien parasite/ the Invisibles/Mind Control block(s) a certain part of our brain or whole area. **He actually states all most every single one of us at one time or another has been affected by this in one way or another.** My daughter was just affected deeply.

Although we know it can leave when the healing has taken place. It has left on occasion, I saw it! That energy has also been completely gone, just like anyone battling something in and out of the body.

There were other ways these Archons and Mind Control have entered into our world besides our Chakra centers: computers, electronics, microwaves, symbolism for our subconscious mind, etc. I continue to explain.

An artificial intelligence can be and is deployed around our planet and in military. The "Cyber Mind" Raven says are what the police of the day are indoctrinated into. They hijack your electrical field. She herself was mind controlled and able to transfer her energy out of the Matrix, as I describe it, and back to herself. She describes, on her talk shows, much of how I see it, or those reclaiming themselves back to Source where nothing can touch them. This is outside the Matrix, as I have been describing. "They will be dictated to" (via electronic airwaves, implants, etc.) Raven says, about the elected politicians, or anyone under electronic harassment or electronic pulses, that they do "PSYCHOTRONIC HITS" that interfere(s) with the TIs or electronically mind controlled/harassed subjects hearing the communication system. Lara, as I have mentioned, always stated her voices as normal communication. "Much of their technology will mimic schizophrenia," she goes on to explain.

The whole field of psychiatry is oblivious to this. I personally see it and hear it all over since I have been doing my research on schizophrenia mimicking mind control and vice versa. Solaris mentions in an interview on one of her shows that Robert Duncan talks about how the technology they have now is so profound that they can mimic schizophrenic brain wave patterns in an EEG. They create a pseudo-symptom pattern of a schizophrenic brain wave, an altered brain wave function so the wave forms on an EEG. will look like schizophrenia when in fact it is a pschyco-tronic weapon or program. I desperately wondered throughout the years before I knew the facts, what the hell else was involved with her mind. **Something, someone was inside her mind, it wasn't just her, I saw it!** Synthetic Telepathy. Neural Linguistic Programming, Psycho-tronic Programming!

I suggest, as well, taking note of Susan Ford and/or now Brice Taylor. She had been a mind control subject for Kissinger and other elites privy to this technology. They used her mind to send messages back and forth to bring out the elites agenda of the NEW WORLD ORDER in the most profound secretive ways through Mind Control, as she states in several of her interviews. You will get a wealth of information. She names "names" of the controllers or handlers that are real people involved, and we would be shocked. She says there are children all over the world being subject to this.

I later found, as I was researching her, discovered a horrifying confirmation based off one of her interviews you will find (If the Internet still remains on in our lives) that at UCLA, here in the States, at the Los Angeles Psychiatric Hospital (they showed the picture of the hospital Lara was in before she was taken away and lost her memory of her family). She allegedly states UCLA/Los Angeles Psychiatric Hospital was or has been working with the CIA involved in these experiments. I cringe when I hear this. I cringe again as the Light Beings confirm this information. I can't tell you how much. I just hope you hear me as well as other parents do and watch her interviews. This is a serious epidemic that is killing our children's minds. I later found the interview with Brice Taylor and Ted Gunderson; please get yourself informed on this. It is crucial. She does a lot of wonderful work with Rosie O' Donnell as well! I bring my child for what I think is help because this is what I as a citizen am directed to do because I wanted the best for my child, to find out the people I am running to for help are the ones also responsible for her condition to begin with. It was sick, it is sick! And we are all involved!

I was certain over and over as I stated in the prior chapter that when Lara was taken from UCLA and transported to LA CASA, there was a strange intervention. You will remember as I wrote in the prior chapters I couldn't get a hold of her during the transfer from UCLA to LA CASA. It took forever and was very mysterious. She then returned not knowing of her identity. The entity residing in her, "Taylor" told me Lara had left during the transfer and was not to return. It was very odd how she was telling me this. My intuition was screaming at myself that something was strange how close she and I were when she went into UCLA. And then during the transfer I was then not recognized by her. Neither was her boyfriend recognized nor her growing baby inside her. Gunderson, in his interviews with Susan Ford states he has had a look at hundreds of confidential files, thousands of pages on Mind Control Experiments that conclude that there are hundreds of unwilling participants from the United States. There was a finding by a Senate investigation that the CIA has indeed conducted experiments on unwilling US citizens; reported in one of the clips that was actually on mainstream television. It states they used CIA allegedly controlled doctors at UCLA.

I again was floored. My intuition and all the information the Light Beings were giving me and continually feeding me, up to this very day, continues to be verified in the physical. It is very hard to digest this. Especially when it is your child. It is so very much more than my daughter. So many parents believe their child is just mentally ill when there is so very much more going on that they are intentionally being withheld from recognizing. I had earlier stated UCLA being one of the best places in the country for help when it came to psychiatry. It perhaps is and that is why I would say the CIA would target the doctors there. Please also listen to the full interview with Brice Taylor and Ted Gunderson titled, "MK ULTRA MIND CONTROL REVEALED." I was astounded that he too also mentioned what you will later read in my letters to the several judges here in Los Angeles at the Edmunds Children Court, that I had learned earlier in the case, about the group called "The Finders" that had existed or still do. We understand, that they purposely hunt for babies and so many others here in the United States to use or sacrifice. The latter letter describes the details as I myself was learning more. This was far more real than my imagination or anger. It was real…I PAUSE, I BREATHE.

Lorien Fenton, who has had regular talk shows on "Revolution Radio" centered wholly around "MIND CONTROL" is as well the founder of the "SUPER SOLDIER SUMMIT." She is a woman that is highly educated and respected on MIND CONTROL subjects. Through her own profound experiences, she has also become aware of mind control and how very real it is. Lorien has interviewed almost everyone taken over by mind control and has had on her show whistle blowers speaking out or people coming forth that have actually worked on the project(s) such as Paper Clip or Project Monarch/ experimentation of the mind. It is worth listening to her archives.

I believe it was her show I was listening to dictating the following: Incidences of the MCS (MIND CONTROL SUBJECTS) are usually when the person is very young. They are much more able to do this when a victim is a "young woman" given a late start. The victim cannot be programmed into alters (alternative realties) but can have her mental activates restricted to their hindbrain (reptilian service) by being kept in a state of extreme fear. The primary personality remains totally unaware of its alters until the slaves programming begins to fail, usually around the age of thirty, which results in severe depression and a mental breakdown for the primary personality. In the interim, if the handler or programmer wants them to use rational brain functions, they can use a preprogrammed trigger to switch them back into their primary personality.

I would like to hone it all into one package here a little clearer. If you have not yet understood how it all relates from the government to mind control to Aliens and our kids, you will in this particular chapter. I explained to you in the previous paragraphs about the technology used in World War II and how it all transpired to mind control. It is important to understand how they are using it today just in upgraded forms, as I have stated throughout the book. Really it is important to understand it is all rolled into one insane topic and that we each understand the correlations. We must do this if we are to help people that have been targeted.

A Light Worker named SKYE

*CLONING

The cloning technology is believed to have come from the supposed Roswell Crash. Aboard ship was information as to "how to" clone people. Certain fashions of government are now masters at cloning not only celebrities but many of our leaders as well as even fake Aliens. In fact they may have even cloned the ship and the aliens in it. An alternate reality is where the possession takes place of the main personality here in our dimension. They clone you in the ethereal and use that clone to manipulate you in reality. Out of nowhere the main personalities will be triggered by the controller using one of their "trigger" moves or suggestions as I stated. The subject will act in bizarre manners depending on what is programmed. The "triggers" can be used to suggest even murder. Many of the mass killing(s) of children are done through these suggestions.

The Archons Network is in general part of the cloning station and vice verse. If the main personality wants to get out they say they will kill them such as believed to be with Whitney Houston. What alarms me, bringing it home, is Lara often screams at me and her boyfriend/father of the baby that we need to stop trying to bring Lara back or she is going to get hurt. She gets mad at us and makes us leave her alone.

A "CLONE" is created, from taking the consciousness, such of what he explains about Britney, in REM sleep and transporting it into the "new body" at the clone center (very similar to what happens in the movie Avatar). Very similar to what happens when someone takes drugs and opens a porthole to a darker realm and the Archons take over via the consciousness or the body. In fact it could be the same thing. I may never know, although the result is the same and it's from the same family. The same family meaning, the dark Kabal taking over our planet by entering into the ethereal. It's just a cousin form of it you could say. Just like chemical trails or vaccines or nanoparticles in our body.

MK Ultra victims, as well as clones, are also programmed into another reality. As I have mentioned the Kabal operates in different realties, different dimensions, and that is perhaps why many Light Workers such as myself have been taken to this timeline.

CHAPTER 12

SETTING "LIVING WITH UNCERTAINTY" INTO ACTION!

I have said to myself over and over again there is no point in doing all this spiritual work and just letting it sit around. One thing I have had to learn, as I often mentioned, and utilize, has been "Living with Uncertainty!" It is difficult to plan anything close to normal. The closest thing to normal was always uncertain. The closest normal sensation of having a grandchild in the making, were the moments I had when I had bought Lara some maternity clothes. I remember going to a few different stores, seeing what was around it was so important to me. I got up early that day like it was such a special day. It really was. I had put back some moments that I have repeatedly been robbed of being the mother of all this

I loved visiting her when she was pregnant. There were time when nature took over and in spite of her mind, her body acted as my child. When I saw her yesterday at her facility she was the prettiest thing ever. Her golden long hair waves itself around her young, pregnant, childlike body during one of our visitations. Her plump cheeks are rosy. There is a glow to her. She smiles big today. She and I hold each other. "I love you my child," I say to her as I always do, always have, and always hope to let her know. Love is the greatest healer on our planet.

A Light Worker named Skye

I put my hands on her belly to say hello to my grandbaby, consciously through loving energy, through my fingers to its presence while it was miraculously preparing itself for arrival. "Are you ready for this baby, honey? You are about to be a mother, and your baby is going to need you to be well." After looking down, she takes a moment to look up at me, stares for a minute and says "I know. Um, yes, Mom, I want the baby." I even recall her saying "mom" as if her higher self had a second to speak. Her delicate blue eyes very seldom show the opening within that longs to surrender, but perhaps I may have noticed a moment, a slight glimmer of her precious heart literally telling me these words as if it had the ability to telepathically speak to me and this is exactly what I heard: "Mommy, I know I'm sick, and I know that you know that I know. Now, please do not get in my way as my disease or my ego must deny this to you. I now know I must put a stop to this. Therefore, my higher consciousness has had to manifest itself in the form of a lockdown facility while I am carrying a child. Perhaps even my child growing inside my disruptive womb has Angels guarding over us both. Know that as much as I am sick, I am connected to this soul beyond unexplainable magical forces. I feel this all inside, mommy. If my mind is asleep, rest assured mommy, my heart awakens to God's voice."

Many times this has happened to me since my daughter's illness took place. In an instant, I had an in-depth sense of my child as if I were connected to her internal spirit. This connection, a sacred bond between mother and daughter, surpasses all understanding and aims directly for its target of knowing its truth.

With my Buddha nature pulling me faster and faster everyday into the arms of wisdom I must finally and strangely say fear not for the Lord is at hand. This was such a valuable lesson. I knew my life could be of much more value to myself if I just stopped worrying about everything. All I did was worry. Worry did not solve an issue for me, and it just puts extra stress on my system while I am trying to sort things out. I must have believed it did do something for me because I kept reaching for it. Worry, or fear, is the exact opposite of the direction needed to get my answers. No problem is solved out of a messy mind. The uncertainty comes from our minds. We want answers so we can prepare for the damage. Life has not been set up that way in the slightest bit. I don't know what ever made us think so. I believe we are given the wisdom to plan something to bring into our world of creation, then manifested. This is then where we let go and let the world play out its plan that includes the all, the One with you. While we observe by the wayside ready to bring the wisdom of love in at any moment as we ourselves were part of creating that which we are now experiencing.

I know during the pregnancy that Lara is not able to take her normal medications. Depakote is harmful for the newborn. Lara's normal medications of Zyprexa mixed with Depakote seemed to have been the medication cocktail that has brought her back from psychosis several times. Although, there is never anything certain when dealing with brain chemistry. The last eleven hospital runs over the past year alone seemed to have done severe damage, as I stated, letting the Archons run the airwaves, literally, or the electromagnetic waves we all share.

Today seemed a bit urgent for me when I arrived at the facility. There is only about a month left of her pregnancy at this point. Another DID disassociation identification disorder, that has continued to surface during her pregnancy, because of the Archon Network and/or the Electromagnetic energy around her body being manipulated, is that she has already had this baby. When I would prompt her back to reality, the reality that she was about to give birth, she would often become agitated. I did not want to push her agitation and cause upset during those visitations but this was a very pressing matter.

We sat under a large fully blossomed tree in the middle of the yard, as I went through each page of the new illustrated baby book I had brought, talking with her about what organs were being developed each month while her baby has been growing. I was emphasizing the words "your," "baby," and "birth." This was the first time she seemed shocked. I watched her face looking at the pictures. At first she seemed to be looking at just some normal book that I was talking about, not much reaction. I could then see her staring at the pages for a minute before her face embellished somewhat of a distorted twitch bringing on agitation halfway through. She suddenly asked me who I was and why I would show her this. I ignored her. I flipped the pages more.

Lara has been disassociated with her body; disassociated from herself. This is the uncertainty that comes with DID. Today, I believe the pictures brought it home for her. I don't have time to see her ill. She recognizes the tones of my voice underneath whatever form of denial her mind takes on.

People with addictions and mental illness (with or without Archons) can be so mortified by their own actions, they create other realities to live in, in order to sideswipe the magnitude of emotions they may feel if they were to actually snap back into the reality of their present existence. It would certainly bring about some emotional earthquakes.

If Lara were to come back to reality, she would have to face a whole lot of things about herself that all along she has refused to face. It may be easier for her to keep the Archon or the illusion around if it serves its purpose. Normally, I would have said here she has to face that she is an addict and she has to face the great destruction she has done in her life. She would also have to face everything that I have had to experience as a result of her addiction, along with whatever needed mending in her life as it is not just about me, either. At her core, I believe, she knows that this may be very hard for her to face. She and I were very close. Her and her boyfriend have a special bond and her unborn is everything she used to grow up wanting.

On this particular visit, during our card game, I had pulled out the notebook I had brought, knowing I could always get a better read with her when she wrote things down. I had her write my name; then hers to keep score for us. First she writes "Skye" as me and "Taylor" as her. Then she crosses it out and writes "Taylor Brown." "Who is Taylor Brown, Lara?" I asked her. She replied, "That's me." I continued asking about Lara and where was Lara, telling her I didn't come here to play games with Taylor. She looks at me and then crosses out Taylor Brown and writes her birth name. She looks at me again and then crosses off Lara and writes Taylor Brown. Taylor was her boyfriend's last girlfriend's first name whom she thought he had been seeing, and Brown is her boyfriend's last name." I still want to know where Lara is," I said. She said she did not know as her voice suddenly became meek sounding, telling me Lara was gone, stating that Lara had hurt a lot of people and caused a lot of trouble everywhere. "She is gone." I did not try to sort out her reality. I just observed it. Then, I explained to her that every single one of us had hurt people and caused trouble and would eventually have to go back inside themselves and face it.

I had a chance to massage her nicely plump pregnant body. It was a very special mother-daughter moment. I was so delighted to see her well nourished during her pregnancy. She was terribly underweight prior to this. Sometimes she feels like I am a stranger touching her and she shies away if I try to hug her. Today, she enjoyed the comfort of my massage and she was letting herself relax. Although, when a fellow patient came up to us she introduced me as her friend "Skye." He asked her if I was her mom.

SETTING "LIVING WITH UNCERTAINTY"...

This time, I told her, my feelings were hurt. There is a point when, if I am triggered in any way, I do address it. I am no example to her to be honest with herself if I am not honest with myself. I did not elaborate. There was no point. I do not need my daughter to validate me in any way in order for me to be at peace with myself, and if I do, I am making her my false God. I am very clear on this interpretation from Source. Although, I did feel disrespected. Again, she does not have to alter herself because I feel disrespected. They are my feelings. She does not give me my feelings. Whatever needs or does not need to be corrected in another is solely between them and the Supreme God. I can only take care of myself in whatever manner I need to.

Source has and will always alter my thoughts of illusions, I believe The Supreme would be eager to rush in and heal any illusions of our world when given an open door. *~It is my only way of manifesting your highest self through you. Your true self is perfect; whole; complete.*~~We only defeat ourselves by asking another to validate us in any way, shape, or form without validating ourselves.~~*If you know yourself as the beauty that you are, the exact beauty of Love itself, you would not need another to repeatedly say anything to you for verifications.*~~This is a dangerous trap used in relationships causing immense and unnecessary heartache.

I used to say to Lara, "See what you have done to me?" as if I needed her to stop in order for me to be at peace; as if I needed her to get well in order for me to live a happy, healthy, full life. I do not need her for anything when I am fully at one with Source. When I am fully at one with Source, all needs are met. "Love thy neighbor as thyself." If you love and care for you first, you will understand the great need to love and care for another. There was a very beautiful message in that that has been so sadly distorted. When we neglect ourselves first, we see a need to neglect others.

Lara neglected herself terribly at the beginning of pregnancy. I did not think that it would go into its ninth month. Everything was so uncertain. Every day was so uncertain. Do I get a crib for this baby, do I get attached to this baby? Is this baby coming home with me even—so many unanswered questions, as I settled into uncertainty day after day.

One big communication system she had for her own body at the time was neglect. Therefore, all she knew was to neglect her unborn, so much so that she denied the very existence of her own child growing inside her. She, still, at this time believes she has had this baby already.

Since this miraculous baby has made its mark on all of our lives, regardless of what its mother thinks or doesn't think about it, what about me? I am hoping I am ready!

How I can be ready for all this? **The same way I had to be ready for every other traumatic thing I have had to go through. I become ready whether I am ready or not. Truth has never been polite to me; it just kind of shows up uninvited.** This miraculous entity that has come to bear life through my child appears to be making a statement in the world, regardless of the conditions before it.

I was asked in the beginning, "Why aren't you having her have an abortion?" as if it were my choice to strap her adult self on a table and have a doctor spread her legs against her will and tear out the baby. That is what that meant. People actually said that to me, "Why aren't you making her get an abortion?" May it always be between the two souls and Prime Creator. It does not matter if the world around would oppose. There never was born a child of mistake. These things do not exist in the mind of the Supreme.

I know all of this, but it is void if not applied. A complete surrender has taken place in my heart. Therefore, my gift back from the Supreme has been our beloved quest and guest…"Peace." Creator has promised each and every one of us freedom when we surrender. Freedom is peace of mind.

The father is ready and anxious although he has his own personal issues. Lara herself does not realize she is about to give birth. Does the soul that we are about to meet come with a body that is unharmed by its mother's life? We live in a world that refuses to let life just be life. A world of uncertainty. There have been so many times in Lara's addiction that I have had the urge to run and get all the pieces underneath together to prevent the falls. I have cleared the space in my head this time for allowing to happen what is going to happen. I have said enough prayers for this situation. I am confident that Source itself is in the middle of this.

I rose early yesterday to take Lara to the doctor's office to check on her growing baby. The staff asked me if I would attend. Lara has refused to honor any doctor's visits concerning her child. She now insists that she has already had the baby. She insists it is with the other children she has had at home. There is no need to go to the doctor. I had her prepped all week with the baby book and verbiage that constantly connected her to her baby. When I arrived at the facility to help escort her for her appointment, the staff informed me that she, again, refused. I firmly then said, "No, get ready, she is going."

The Supreme took over me, and all fear was cast aside. I knew she was going. My intuition was in charge, not me. She had denied treatment every time, but I knew this particular time she was going. Sometimes fear can override my knowingness, but I did not waiver. I had a clear message that this child was going to find its care regardless of its mother's unwillingness and it did. It made sure it was taken care of even before its birth. It knows its glory before its arrival from the spirit world. I know this. The baby knows this. The sadness comes when we, as human beings, lose our connection to Source the minute we are aware of the energy of the collective consciousness in this dimension.

The consciousness of this dimension has over time greatly depleted its awareness of its natural state. Under love, there is no definition of fear. It is that simple, yet complex for the human mind. This is its great message given to us. It is calling us back to receive this message one by one, one person at a time. Each heart must know its truth. There is no lack in the mind and heart of the Supreme. This soul knows its connection to its true nature. I know my connection to my true nature, for it has shown me its life firsthand through mine, and I commit to this source. If I know this true nature and you know this true nature, and every other soul did imagine the world, this would be. Imagine the world that your child and my child could grow up in.

CHAPTER 13

GROWING UP WITH MENTAL ILLNESS.

MY LIFE THEREAFTER!

Each cycle of **my** life has been critically affected as a direct result of people I love or grew up with who had mental illness or addictions, addictions that either had Archons attached with them or addictions controlled by the dark, starting with my childhood, continuing into young adulthood.

I came into this planet with this softness or this understanding of the heart, the god-essence. It was embedded in me. I believe that softness comes from the Planet I am from, different then here. My mother used to say I was sweet. The word "sweet" my ego used to hate. I couldn't understand why everyone else wasn't sweet and noticing how I was seemed odd to me, an insult that meant I was somehow weak.

I started my initial seeking for answers to life at a very young age after a childhood with a very troubled mother who, from what I saw, was expressing her extreme depression and chemical imbalances in the form of violence, alcoholism, or even a bipolar/split personality disorder, with its "mania" being on the violent side rather than manifesting its mania as signs of grandiosity. I first started to learn of mental illness through my mother. There is a difference, I see, between mental illness and having an Archon fully take over the body and or an occasional leech or one that is being electronically mind controlled. I know I have lived with a person with mental illness, my mother.

GROWING UP WITH MENTAL ILLNESS...

My mother's way of dealing with her depression often showed its dark colors. I recall the terror I felt by her methods of discipline of locking me in our cellar as a form of time out. The only place you could go was the dark, cold cellar. Usually about the same time, she was using my very young, tender wrists, biting them as hard as she could or at least until decently bruised; at best, breaking the skin for its arrival of blood for the purpose of unnecessary dominance over a delicate, petite child. She sent me to my Catholic school several times with black and blue marks and welts up and down my body. All the while, we attended her church of faith every Sunday of our lives. These were among the many stories of her insanity. Actions like this are usually when there is a Leech attaching. These Leeches are far more prevalent in such violent acts that are not of true human nature, although I will repeatedly explain that the negative energy cannot live in a body full of Christ, my mother later became redeemed by her savior and has committed her life to Jesus as she sees fit. I look back and wonder what kind of people we were as a whole and wonder where the message of growing up with nonviolent communication was missed.

Of course, the salvation I was to find from such an upbringing before my mother's healing was to gravitate toward the like vibrations of such violence as I met my daughter's father. I remember one time (among many) he locked my pregnant body inside our barely furnished, older wooden apartment during the pregnancy, asserting his presence over me, reminding me that he did indeed, at that time, have power over me as he was so claiming to have had during his violent rages. I couldn't get out. I ran to the bathroom for refuge. I was taken back by a knife to my throat while my daughter's body and its pure essence picked up the violence during its stay in my womb. I later learned how much of a breath those incidents were for the Archons. I was keeping them alive; not only through my terror but also the life force energy growing inside me.

As I stated at the beginning of the book, this was my usual home life during pregnancy as a young adult. You can perhaps see why it was so easy for me to take that ride from the stranger that I did when I waiting for my usual ride home from work. I used to lay in the tub and soothe my stomach when I could and talk to this growing baby, telling her how much I loved her and everything was going to be okay one day. I always said this baby growing in me kept me alive because I loved her so much and felt the need to protect her though very unable to love and protect myself like this. How could I? I had zero training on self-love. Lara was my gift from the get-go. To look at her as anything but, to this day, is my own erroneous thinking, she has made me the strong vibrant woman I am. She was and is my gift to recognizing that I am a Light Worker on a very special mission.

When I had let Lara's father into my young adulthood, he was like a sober prince, before his drug relapse from his own admitted addiction to crystal meth, with **periods,** not permanent, of paranoid schizophrenic delusions himself. He had a super strong spiritual twelve-step program with excessive knowledge of the unknown, of aliens and ETs, etc., that immediately captivated me. The brief time he maintained the life of sobriety, I fell deeply in love and became pregnant, not knowing this strong prince would ever relapse.

I was thankful for the strong ties I was making back then as well as the strong ties I was making in the metaphysical world. I am eternally grateful for the endless wealth of knowledge I have picked up from that experience. It whipped me into shape so fast in life. I never once dated or attracted a man again who laid a hand on me. I also became a determined, powerful, strong woman. He forced me into self-worth, when I had had enough.

CHAPTER 14

THE PROCESS OF LETTING HER GO TO LOVE

Feelings of anxiety rush through my veins as my mind trembles to sort out what I can and can't save with my daughter, and what kind of mother people think I am. "Oh, my god. What happens if I can't save this at all? What happens if all this really is something I have no control over?"

I always thought that I had a certain amount of control over things if I loved them and willed them into life. I do actually have control over my dominion; but it is my dominion, not hers. I have come to understand that my daughter is someone I have no control over. This process did not happen overnight. In meetings we often talk about everything being a process and progress rather than perfection. It felt like I had control when she was younger because I was in charge of things. I ran things; not people; and I did have control of some things. Although you can plan plans, but you cannot plan results. I planned on my daughter having an amazing life, and the truth is she still might or might not, but she still might. She is very young, but it is not my choice. I don't care how much I fight it. It is 100 percent OUT OF MY CONTROL. For some reason, it has been one of my hardest lessons to grab, especially because I know the God code and the way to integrate "God Energy" into my life and manipulate energy around me. Therefore, I thought that I should have been able to manipulate that of my daughter's. In fact, for me to conquer another life's path to fit my scenario is crossing the path of the Supreme. I would hate it if my mother was trying to conquer my path and plotting things with God to have things go her way.

A LIGHT WORKER NAMED SKYE

It is important to understand energy. You are a Creator God, moving energy at all times. Do not forget this. Praying for one to access the god self is always sending the appropriate energetic signal out to the universe.

My body cringed every step of the way having to accept that this was something I could not fix. I knew practically everyone there was to know here in Los Angeles to fix things. I have tons of in(s) with the Creator Gods. I communicate with Masters on all levels. I have access to our energy codes on our planet, and I can't fix her. I had all the knowledge you could muster up: twenty-six years of Al-Anon and tons of program therapy; endless research on drugs and alcohol, schizophrenia, mental breaks, psychosis, Archons, chemicals, pills, treatments, recovery centers, and on and on and on. It makes not one bit of difference. I am telling you if this could be fixed, I would have fixed it; period; end of story.

It is interesting how long it took me to realize I did not have control of her life and her disease. I did not have control over her Archons. I was forced into letting Lara go because I, myself, wasn't going to. I was literally forced out of her life. It was as if God could not have spelled the word "STOP" right in front of my face. I could not accept that this was her life and that where she is in life is not okay. I actually dislike very much when I do this. It is like me saying that life does not have the pieces together and that the Supreme (life cycle energies) management of her life is off.

I laugh when I hear myself say that because God's source management of me was never off. It took every bit to get me to surrender in life the way that I did. I can't imagine what it would be like for someone else's life, but that is it. I cannot imagine. I am not supposed to imagine what anyone else's private reuniting with their Creator looks like. Each soul will without a doubt reunite with their Creator. How long they take the separate ride is a very personal plan between that soul and the higher realms. It is a plan and a contract between them and Creation, and this contract does not have my name on it. For whatever reason an Artificial Intelligence, Mind Control God or just plan life, I am being stopped, forced to let go.

Perhaps, the unbearable cross many parents have to bear is the cross of letting our daughters or sons fall and not knowing how far down or where they are going to land, if they even do….

That's right. I did not know how far she was going to fall or if there was a landing at all The problem for me was that the further she fell is all the more room I had to dip in.

THE PROCESS OF LETTING HER GO TO LOVE

When I first wrote this title down, I wrote "letting her go." That just did not cut it. It will never be something that I just let go of. It is a process: a big process. One of the hardest things to do is to let go. It is an overused cliché to me but it is used over and over for a reason. Through time, it seemed as though the definitions of love changed greatly. Therefore, the definition of letting go came in cycles. Loving her as a child seemed much different than loving her as the mother of a drug addict. Loving her as a drug addict seemed much different than loving her as a mind controlled or mentally ill girl. Loving her as the mother of an Archon named Taylor Brown rather than Lara was even a very different loving. Each of them had their challenges. The child and teenager were a challenge because we were alone and both vibrant beings. Though it once was a beautiful innocent mother/daughter journey, it was a journey that was boldly robbed and interrupted (like so many other parents now) by the violent storms of the other versions of her and her Archon(s) and/or coupled with electronic harassment and/MK Ultra.

I have lived through all of the possible ways a parent could love a child. I believed in love so much that I thought it would do anything; especially save my daughter. I knew how to bring love to each of the ways a mother of a sick child can love; the psychosis, or electronically controlled girl, the addict, the lost mind, the daughter, the daughter that's not my daughter (as she says); the girl that was tons of fun in every way possible!

I didn't understand how all that love and all the education my daughter had grown up with, knowing the twelve-step programs and all the metaphysic churches I brought her to…all the years of spiritual groups that wouldn't have prevented such a fall. I didn't understand. I did not understand how someone who had all that I did not could fall like this. I just couldn't grasp what the reason was. Day in and day out I have surrendered with my head held high and my body crumbling forward telling you what I know to be true…People do fall from grace. This is the glory of the planet we are on, the gift of evolving; an evolutionary planet; a spiritual evolutionary planet. It is a playground to work out our missions to one day recognize our own God-self. I have been shown this without mistake. Therefore, I now also learned that I was to trust. I was to shut my mouth and to trust while she develops her God-self regardless of appearance in the outer world.

A Light Worker named Skye

I learned to trust that everything was, is, and always will be for a higher purpose. I let go in pieces. I let go and I take back. The process goes on until contentment reaches the body and the mind. Contentment eventually will flutter over a broken, shattered world; all things are made anew in the light. All things are possible, even letting go; letting go of outcomes; letting go of anger; letting go of control, and finally letting go of the "fear" that ran everything.

Holding this truth, long enough, until the gentle voice can come into being and melts with the wisdom and contentment of creation within. May we understand all things are made in God's creation for all things come back to Source. In freeing, we find contentment. Knowing without a doubt that Source is at hand, knowing without a doubt that the original God molecule resides within the addict, and the original God molecule will always win, seen or unseen.

Each step of the way the concept of setting her free (from my bondage) seemed to take on a new meaning. When the reasonable type of management of the unmanageable did not work anymore, I started to understand that I was losing my imagined control. It was like I was watching things that were still somewhat in the management stages become unmanageable. I had to slowly fight, kick, and scream, practice and learn to let go of the results. It was confusing because I was seeing the loss of control of being a parent and my mind being a parent wanted to control. I wanted to control outcomes. I had to let go of the fact that I had no control over her disease. This didn't mean I was letting go of doing parental actions and making rules. This meant that she decided not to follow what I said and how I ran things. As time went on, I had to let go of my need to have things a certain way in order for me to be okay. If I were to base my happiness on if she followed my rules or not, I would have been doomed with unhappiness.

Toward the middle of the addiction, it was things like "Well if she gets picked up by the cops I'll have to let go, step aside, and let her suffer the consequences." This is how I eventually learned to deal with this. I got lots of practice too with the cops always coming over. So much so I had went out on a date with of them once one time, it seemed like it was the prime of my social life! Although now I do not even look at it like she has to suffer the consequences. I am starting to capture some clarity on the bigger picture.

This is not about making her suffer to please me and making her get better, so I don't have to struggle with the horrible effects of addictions (although that would be nice). This is a struggle that goes far beyond what that would mean for her. Rather than focusing on her suffering and consequences that are not my business will remain between her and her Creator. I am taking a moment to grab my power back. Instead of this being about her, maybe I should ask myself how I can cope with the ever changing battles I encounter on an ongoing basis in life that seem to rob me of my serenity. Yet, it isn't just about that either. As I dig deeper I see there is always more than one gift of wisdom brought from each set of tragedies.

CHAPTER 15

DETACHMENT

The gift of detachment; detachment without a doubt is a gift of freedom. Once you touch this kind of freedom you may be inclined to keep it for life. Detachment is letting go of the crazies; the crazy feelings; the crazy scenarios that play out; the crazy worries; the crazy way of trying to manage the unmanageable…and then, imagine not feeling it all and just loving the person, not the actions of the person. Imagine not being attached to outcomes or results and breathing in freedom. We learn that we can let go of what one is doing and just trust that LIFE/Source has things playing out in a manner that is and we have no control over this. It is also in a manner that is suitable for them, not us. I want my daughter to learn lessons on my time frame so that my effects can be lessened, but she doesn't. I wanted her to be better for so many holidays I missed with her but she wasn't. I wanted her to be better to see all the events I did in life, but she wasn't. I wanted her to be proud of me for…but she wasn't. I wanted her to be better so that I didn't have to experience the way that my grandchild came into the world, but she wasn't. She did not do what I wanted her to do because I was in pain and it meant so very much to me. Detachment allowed me to not take it personal. It is a golden tool.

CHAPTER 16

BLAMING THE PARENTS !
THE IGNORANCE SOCIETY
OWNS

What kind of mother am I to have watched her fall to such great lengths as she did and not be able to catch her? I have been asked more than once how could I let my daughter get like this, as if I am God; as if there is no interference of God's will in this realm. As I mentioned, I used to get so sensitive about this. I believed that it was my fault too. I actually believed because I raised her, I alone was responsible for how she turned out. This gives no merit to Creation, to life, to her spirit, her biology, to chemistry, to her DNA, to society's influence, which are all more the pieces of the whole than I had being her mother!

People want someone to blame. This is the natural reaction. Usually, it's the parents that someone targets so that their own mind can make logic sense of something that is not logical. The times in my life when I have had issues with people for whatever reasons, having a daughter being mentally ill and on drugs or taken over, was their perfect tool to attack me with. They had always made it known that they thought Lara was crazy because of me, in order to induce whatever charge they had over me. I have to remember that if I wasn't sensitive about this, it wouldn't have been used. It is amazing to me what blindfolds the world puts on to what is really going on. If we can figure out who to blame, then we can figure out what to fix or omit. Therefore, the problem is solved according to the logic mind. It couldn't be any further from the truth. The problem cannot be fixed by the logic mind, or it would have been fixed by now. I, too, was one of those people. I've search endlessly for answers that the mind is incapable of comprehending.

It's interesting to deal with other people's reactions to my daughter's illness. It can be delicate at times to balance my emotions with the emotions of others around my daughter who love her as well. Most of the time we all share the same frustrations in trying to sort everything out. It is an interesting balancing act to go through; all the other family members' reactions to Lara's illness/take over in the mix, as well as my own. The charge behind most people's reactions to a loved one can be profound. Everyone wants to rush in to fix everything up really quick. It's amazing to see that I was not the only one to react this way when I first learned of my daughter's take over/ illness. Some are very quick to point out what they would have done different. I found it quite amusing that the people who never have had a child themselves seem to have the most advice. I found it quite interesting to catch the weight of the thoughts lingering: "Well I told you so. If you only had that girl under control…" seemed to be the vibe sometimes thrown my way. No one really knew how to take in the account of mental illness/MK Ultra/electronic harassment; everyone wants to blame someone.

Although, someone will look at it like my daughter is a crazy undisciplined girl and it must be my fault somehow. I have had to hold my head up high so many times in those spots absolutely knowing that underneath someone's thought was probably the thought that I am somehow at fault. I have had to set my pride aside and bless the person with the sweet comments, knowing that there is no way possible anyone could ever know what this is like. Even if I were to know all the answers, it still would have not changed things. I am convinced that if Lara had another mother and another father and grew up in another home completely different than what I had offered, she still would have ended up this way. This journey is about her, just like my journey is about me. No matter what she does, she cannot walk my path for me. Likewise no matter what I do I cannot walk her path for her.

CHAPTER 17

ANXIETY

N othing would calm down my anxiety. Nothing. I would toss and turn at night. I couldn't breathe. I would worry, and it took huge amounts of sedative pills to bring me to the zero point where I could figure out what to do next. Seemed like I was always wanting a Vicodin, or a Narco, or a Xanax, or an Ativan. It also took large amounts to tame me. I look back and wonder how I stayed alive. I was drinking quite a bit of wine, and I was deathly depressed. I remember taking pills to sleep with alcohol, not even caring that the two together were dangerous, until I had a couple of hallucinations of my own. Thank God or my Guardian I was in safe hands the one or two times it did happen. Nowadays I don't even like to take aspirin, I tell everyone that the pills back than I took all went to the mental pain. It literally sucked the energy out of any pill as if to just get me back up to the zero point. I never really felt distorted. I just felt normal back up at zero; I was so very far down. I also took antidepressants as if they were life support. I don't understand how my body handled all that. It really does not like poisons in it. It never has. Although, when I was running around trying to fix my daughter, I neglected terribly myself. Everything weighed on me. I hated living with the mental torment. I hated feeling responsible, but I didn't even know I had a choice not to. It never occurred to me that I could even try to give myself permission not to take responsibility for her disease. I was her mother. I was responsible. That's all that could compute in my brain. It never occurred to me that I actually could work with my body and calm the anxiety either, but there was and is a way and it is possible, I just didn't know it.

A Light Worker named Skye

I was scared to let go of the guilt and anxiety. I felt like it meant that I okayed everything. If I stopped wanting it different, then that meant I accepted things the way that they were. Furthermore, I could not accept things the way they were. If I did, then that meant I could not have gone back in time to correct it. Therefore, if I hold on to trying to see what went wrong, I might get an answer that will somehow make it better today. On and on, my mind went. It was this whirlwind game between accepting the way things were and trying to change what was.

Chapter 18

GUILT;

the Choices i had to Make Along the Way!

I would write songs about life that would help me sort things. I put together bands and created albums of work that meant almost everything to me. It gave life a purpose and kept me reaching for more. It allowed me to sort out my thoughts in ways that otherwise would have probably killed me with my powerful charge of emotions. I would duel in thought, thinking I should have been home with her the few of nights I went to rehearsal instead of being with my band. I still wished I was there because I loved her and loved being home with her or at least I wished for her a healthy father being there or a family member, but that wasn't our story. To this day, I will tell you that taking care of myself via creative expression was what kept me alive to show up and be her mother to begin with. I have learned to relax with myself more about this and to melt into what was. In fact, I have learned to honor who I was and how I went to the creative arts to express myself, and that was that.

Should I have disciplined her more? I whirled in this forever. Was my loving way of mothering the exact opposite of what she needed? I actually say yes to both of those as I look back to where this all went wrong. Now what? I can't go back. We don't get a second chance at raising that particular soul and all that comes with them. We also give so much false duty to them nurturing our own unhealed wounds. I remember hearing my daughter's cries and running to comfort her as if it was me crying; feeling my childhood pains that I did, running to comfort myself. I saw how clearly I played out my own emotions and feelings. I could have had a more balanced perspective, correcting the direction of things if they weren't my cries that I was hearing.

That wasn't my story, though, as I had learned to forgive myself. Except for my basic care, I had a horrible childhood in many ways. How could I have known a healthy balanced way to raise a child myself? In fact, I started to really realize how much love my daughter received and what a great life she really did have, in spite of how hard my childhood was. I really picked up the pieces and moved forward, providing a decent life for us. I also started to go a bit easier on my mother, understanding she, too, did the best she could with the knowledge she had and how her brain computes things. Instead of blaming my mother, my thoughts would go more toward compassion for mothers. It is hard to be a mother. It is one of the honored roles to mankind for a reason.

One of my therapists throughout the years said to me that the facts are whether a child comes from a single family home, a disciplined home, or a structured home, or a spiritual home, an addict is an addict. I know that line repeats itself but an addict is an addict. Period. I get it now.

Slowly, through time, I understood I could start to use my story for good and claim the strength that I need whenever needed. This became a very powerful gift to me from the "Light Beings." It was truly a gift. It was something that allowed me to turn poison into medicine, as we say in the Buddhist meetings I go to.

Being in Hollywood and being in entertainment, I was really geared toward looking good. When I was younger, in my early teens and early adulthood, for a brief period I was battling somewhat of a minor weight issue brought on by an extreme inner void. I did not know anything about my feelings being associated with how much I ate. I grew up a ballet dancer. I was always in shape, working hard, and performing. At the point of transitioning into adulthood, I had no idea how to handle what I ate or took in my body. Everything I did in my life was because I was either beaten into doing it or by routine. I never learned to just listen to my body, to eat when I was hungry and stop when I was full (until years after I had my daughter). The older I got the more the wounds started to heal about my body, and as I grew as a person, the desire to take care of my body became like an art of love. I learned everything there was to learn about nutrition because I was worth it. I initially went on a six-month diet and lost the thirty-five to forty extra pounds of "protection" I had through exercise and commitment, but most of all I was amazed that changing my thoughts and loving myself was the only diet I ever needed. I continued to care for my body and took much pride in it. I came very much into honoring my body and allowing it to flourish into fantastic shape. I loved that I relinquished this pain from my life. Back then, kids in high school were outrageously mean about weight. It used to torture me, I remember. As an adult, I dove into health and shaped my body into a very powerful state of being. I live by a vegan diet and exercise to relieve the enormous amounts of energy that comes zooming through my body at unexpected times. The shape my body was in coupled with the breast implants that I had decided to give myself for my fortieth birthday and being in the entertainment field all allowed me to morph into a body type that was very powerful for a female with cosmopolitan appeal. I had often wondered if my disposition, that of being in a rock band wearing flattering clothes threatened my daughter. I had to look at that, too. I had to look at everything that lingered in my mind. I hated looking at that. I was very defensive on being me, but I had to look at everything. That was the promise I had given myself. At first, I felt ashamed that I wasn't a soccer mom type. My guilt even took control over my perceptions of self. I didn't know who I was supposed to be, really. There are many things that I could have done differently, but if there is no acceptance of self, then there is a barrier for God's creative-force energy to come in and transform where needed. Likewise, if there is a self that needs to be transformed, it will be transformed through being honest with self in any given moment. This truth -vibration will automatically cleanse the self into the higher self. It is a foolproof system the truth will set you free.

I later wasn't worried about who I was and who I became. I could only be me. I erroneously thought that if I was a different type of person, my daughter would be different. I also thought that if I needed changing, the Holy Spirit would get in there and do its work on me. Although most of what I learned was that the Supreme had me right where I was supposed to be. Why would I want to change me, and why would I be arrogant enough to label one look, (a soccer mom look) to look better than any other look (a fit body) to be better or worse for a child? Again I was believing that something external had control. The amount of daily repair to keep up with my daughter's addiction was getting beyond a full time job. I had to stay home from working full time in the spa at that time as a licensed aesthetician, another place I heard many precious stories in life; also, a place where great healers were brought my way to deal with what I needed too. Mother, Father God works everywhere in life. At home, I was always focusing my energies on getting us out of the immediate crisis or danger we were in. Point in mind, at one point, Lara had been involved with a couple of gang members here in LA. If you know LA, you know that is not pretty. That was in the last place I lived before I knew I had to get out of my living situation with her. It was before I had to make to the most heart wrenching most difficult decision of my entire life being a parent, to move and not have my own precious daughter know where I lived. I have followed through with that, that is why she had nowhere to go except for the hospital to get help. It killed me, oh God that was so hard for me, but I could see it, - it may have killed her to have enabled her by living with me.

I was being threatened, emotionally terrorized. I had to sleep with the couch next to the window for a long period of time and wake up every ninety minutes to check on things. She owed money and had caused other commotion. I was terrified. I had reached points right past the fear and became very powerful; very brave; almost like a mother bear protecting her cub. I believe God intentionally gave me a great dose of that kind of energy. I don't believe I am unique in that nature.

Three years into my daughter's addiction while she was still a minor, it was becoming impossible for me to keep a job and take care of her. I took a free-lance project producing a "B" movie here in Hollywood with a very interesting, intense director who had intense issues, both physically and mentally. The movie was bizarre and kept my mind whirling, trying to manage everything and take my mind off my daughter although that did not happen. My daughter continued her dysfunction. I recall having a few cast and crew members over to do a location shot at my house because the outside and the patio area looked like something he had stuck in his head to film. My daughter was in the bedroom up on the bed in some protruding bizarre position, half dressed while talking out loud, as if answering her controllers, in some strange manner that alarmed the hell out of me. It was awful to see, I felt that pit in my stomach seeing her and watching those controllers. I stopped her and yelled at them as to leave her alone. One of the actors tried to calm her down so he could do the scene.

Guilt; the Choices I had to Make...

When she was finally calm, we would just switch to another scene while she was at the kitchen faucet screaming, "Get off me!" as the sound guy flies up from sitting on the couch. He stops dead in his tracks to witness this. I had forgotten how bizarre her behavior was in general because I lived with it so much; I couldn't see it. She screamed, "Get off me!" a few times. I wondered who she was screaming that to. This in and of itself was and is another confirmation of Electronic Harassment/Mind Control. The center of my being would just peel over in disgust and hurt. It was very hard to step back from the fact that when she was in danger, I was powerless.

Shortly after filming the movie where others had to witness my daughter's behavior, the neighbors there, in the private off-street backspace that I had, were really getting agitated at my daughter screaming insane things off the balcony. I was becoming beyond exhausted trying to manage her. I had just moved from the three-bedroom home we had because I could not manage her, the animals, the yard, and the house. Again, I had to downsize to manage this whole thing. I hated where we had to live, but I needed an area that was somewhat lax. We found a home where the cops visited often, and most of the neighbors minded their own business (probably because they were all illegal immigrants and they did not want any problems themselves). Nonetheless, I was exhausted and run ragged. I could not manage anything anymore. The director of the film was trying to arrange another scene at my new place, and I was going way beyond my limit of what I could handle. Lara was on a run every day or every other day. The mental illness was full blown. The new neighbor behind me was a kind older lady with diabetes who could see the enormous stress I was under. I would sit outside and smoke the cigarettes that I so dearly was trying to quit every day at the time. She would see me with my self-help books or doing my morning prayers as I desperately was trying to hang onto life. We would often talk as she took a liking to Lara's dog and was very concerned about him. She ended up taking him as yet another move had to be arranged. My life was falling apart. I couldn't manage Lara. I had no money and no way out that seemed manageable for me. One thing I did have was survival skills and I had to use them. Despite her being sick and life being a wreck, the bills still had to be paid.

I had a friend who was a topless dancer in Las Vegas who knew my situation and connected me to what I needed to know to get there and make some money so I could keep the bills going. I never really had issues around this type of thing back then. I was oblivious to the Archons. In a way, I was thankful for that back then. I grew up in a very strict Catholic school whose nuns spanked you when you were bad. I used to hold an overabundant amount of shame around sexuality. Nowadays, after I met the light and the Light Beings and had my Kundalini experience, the vibration of that whole world would not work for me whatsoever. I can't even tolerate a nightclub. Though, at the time, I was more nervous and excited. It was Vegas.

The club I got hired in was one of the top elite clubs that hired some of the prettiest girls on the planet, making top dollar. I was older and competing with much younger girls. I was thankful I looked the way I did; I blended well, regardless of their age. I loved dancing once I got there. I knew enough about the whole dark side of that world to approach it as a job. Expressing myself, topless or not, is utterly beautiful, I thought to myself, not to mention empowering. I loved to dance, I felt powerful I was trained to feel power as a dancer, I love(d) to dance and call on the inner power of the Goddess. I loved climbing the pole and flipping upside down as if to capture alternate views. I had conversations with some of the richest men in the world, one of them owned an entire country! Another fantastic place to get the real truth about what's going on in people's homes. I learned so much about men. They told me everything. It was odd but the men that picked me would have conversations about deep topics in life. Many men, surprisingly enough, had frustrations that they could not get out in their personal lives, so they'd come to the club for solace. Having a topless woman dance next to them and converse while they have a few drinks seemed to have worked for some. Some became my regulars. Especially in Fargo, North Dakota, a few friends and I from Los Angeles and Las Vegas would fly out to this place called The Northern. It was a happening place. Girls from everywhere would travel there. The guys were sweet as pie, hard working men who had great manners and much generosity. My regulars would sit and listen to me talk about my daughter, as that is all I talked about. I remember I would fight back the tears from each customer while I would talk about her. I remember one guy sat there and paid for my time as I frantically called her back in Los Angeles. Right before I left, there were a series of things that happened that led Lara to one of her several rehabs. During her stay, where she had actually run into one of the girls she had gone to elementary school with (interesting how their energies continued to gravitated toward one another), she and a few other girls decided to jump out the window and escape. Lara was 17. I had instructed the sweet lady behind me, Barbara, that I would be gone, so naturally she was on guard. When Lara and her friends broke into my home, Barbara called the cops when she heard the shatter of my living room window while they barged in and invaded my home. Upon my return, I walk into a boarded up window, shattered glass, and a note from police being sent to Children Services wondering why my minor daughter was alone. I was beside myself. When Barbara told me what happened she started that one of the guys Lara was with was also being arrested for something, and between all of them, they had the helicopters circling my home before they escaped. The place was a mess. It felt dirty and was smoky. I recall the thick residue of energy left in the room. I went to my back area to relax, check my e-mails, and absorb everything that had just happened. I sat down at my desk and noticed it was quite bare. They took it. Apparently, my daughter's friends stole my computer. I was crushed. I ran to my smoking prayer table (at the time) and balled. I was so exhausted from my trip. It's not the highest vibration to be around and coming back to this was a dear tear to my heart; all of my work; all of my pictures. Some very private things, including personal pictures, documents from a small aroma therapy business I had, songs I had written and recorded through the years; pictures of us. I was so distraught. I would take seven or eight Vicoden over several hours and easily drink a bottle of wine throughout the day again just to get my nerves back up to the zero point.

I had to make extra trips that month to the club in Vegas to manage the repair work. Once, I took Lara and her guy friend. Actually, he seemed okay. She was a wicked wreck. I had to work the evening shift and told my daughter and her friend I was performing as in singing and dancing. It was not unlike me to perform, so that was not unusual only not that kind of performance and not in Vegas. She had kept me up nonstop on some kind of crazy meth and or mind run. She was so off that the security guard kept bringing her back to the room. I was on zero sleep and tons of unhealthy sleeping pills that did not work and only kept me up. I am surprised I did not collapse the other nights at work. The alcohol and dancing kept me going in a strange, ethereal way. I loved to dance to the music; to an audience it always tapped me into something euphoric. The dancing covered up the severe life condition I was in and the immense pain I felt over my daughter.

A Light Worker named SKYE

I also met girls on my level in that whole world, too, who struggled with similar issues in life, and these girls were not phony girls. They talked to me. They were girls dying inside with their own struggles just like I was. God's message is everywhere. There were also girls that were nowhere near on that plane. I used to blame myself for being in that whole business as if I wasn't supposed to give myself permission to be who I was and learned what I learned.

I tried to read every author from every spiritual seminar or guru or philosophy there was to read if I hadn't read them yet, oddly enough during my trips that lasted eight months. It made me stay connected to my soul. When I was in Vegas I used to sit for hours in clearing meditations and cleanse my body and mind from the toxins of the lower worlds I was engaged in. It was quite interesting that the second I was done with infusing myself to Mother Father God, I went to the lower world, and the second I got out of the lower world I went right to God Source. It was an interesting duality we are all faced with in many ways, I believe. Everyone has a yin and a yang. It is by design. It is a creation within itself. We use the darker side to get to the higher. Many occult religions will tell us this. They do it and we do it in our own way. Our ego or our lower nature gets us into trouble to clean out of us what is needed to clear out of our psyche by creating chaos and bringing it to the surface to clear out.

I also had a life at the time where I could not miss one second of my connection to Source being the mother of someone with my daughter's issues and how much I needed the assistance and guidance. Because of my constant connection to Source, I kept a very proper home life, and because I cared dearly of the precedence I had in front of my daughter, I carried myself in a loving way. I never really had guys overnight or moving in and out of the house. My home was kept nice and very spiritual because I was a nice, spiritual person. I never had drugs at my house nor alcohol unless there was an occasion. My home was very much like my heart and I kept it that way because I had a child. Eventually, through some tough work with my program, spiritual counselor, and ex-boyfriend, I released myself from that entire short lived adult world years ago and never looked back. I blessed it for what it was and how very much I learned about myself.

I asked myself in retrospect how could I have felt guilty for all this. Oddly, I got some of all the crucial lessons I needed in life right there. There couldn't have been a more appropriate place. It was all based in the major life lessons I needed and had absolutely no way of acquiring, if not for every ounce of experience I absolutely had to live through in order to gain the experience. **You cannot teach experience**. I learned boundaries; physical boundaries where you can and can't touch me, what I can and can't do that is okay or not okay for me sexually. Where else would I perfectly learn what it is needed to learn about my own personal boundaries but in a place where they are constantly being tested? I was made to have physical boundaries. I was taught to be a good girl when I was younger and shut my real voice out and take orders. I was on a perfect path to become a very powerful woman who knew the glory of honoring her body in such a wonderful way because I knew the opposite of what it was like not to. I learned boundaries that stuck for life. I needed those years to become the woman I am. Why in god's name would I, for one minute, question my life and feel guilty for where God had me?

There are, indeed, many things I could have done differently. Another therapist reminds me that my intentions were of pure love every step of the way. Even when we have the best intentions, we must admit our powerlessness of addiction and our powerlessness over life's plan with another individual.

I have been shown that we pick the life condition we enter into once we take our place on earth. Lara picked me as her mother and had to deal with whatever life condition it was she needed to gain the agreement she had with her soul and what it needed to work out. I was part of that plan. I once asked her why she picked me, when she was at the state where I knew her own higher self could understand the depth and the dimensions of the question and she said, "Because I knew you would take care of me!" I remember that so clearly.

A Light Worker named SKYE

There isn't anything that torments the heart of a mother like her own personal guilt. We are instinctively wired to protect our young. If something went wrong, we automatically believed we did our job in error. It is all about how we did or did not do something that caused this. We are responsible for the love and care we give them. We protect them. We still see them as those babies we took home from the hospital, and it becomes embedded in our being. We believe we are responsible from that point on because we birthed them. Every cut, bruise, or heartache, we wonder where could we have protected them. To this day, when I have a natural moment of fighting what is, I always say to myself things like, "God, if I just didn't bring her to Los Angeles"; "if I married that one guy"; "if I had more of a back bone"; or if I made this choice or that choice, depending on what is lingering in my mind. I always found a way to put myself into the equation of why she was sick. My mind was still acting as if it could figure it all out. Perhaps this or that would have been the very thing that would have made it all different. This one funny lady I would see around meetings though the years used to say in a very high pitched, funny tone, "Thank God one of the slogans isn't 'to figure it all out'!"

It took years of therapy and working with the best spiritual practices I had to tame my mind from wishing I did things different. I heard another lady speak at an Al-Anon meeting stating that she said to herself, "What did I do? What did I do?," and her higher voice just reminds her that that was the best she could do. That's what she did. The first year, I was swarmed with guilt. It felt like it lingered over my being and weighed me down. I found myself almost apologizing for being a mother to people. I was so humiliated. I remember that it took so long in the meetings to say my daughter was an addict/taken over. This is even after years of programs. For some reason, I found it much harder to admit I was the mother of an addict rather than a daughter or a girlfriend. I am not sure why. It's not like you can cause a disease to happen in one person and not the next. My logical mind did not make sense when it came to guilt. I was her mother. Therefore, I was guilty. No one else raised her. I was supposed to teach her everything, and if she didn't get it, it was something I did, my mind continued to believe. I felt responsible for everything.

The world centered on my choices. Therefore, my choices made another act a certain way or not. It is quite amazing to learn that my daughter's soul has its own path and its own journey whether I am her mother or not. I took it all on though. My mind still said that I educated my daughter and had her grown up in meetings, support groups, and spiritual groups. I was the one who was going to control the outcome with my knowledge. It didn't occur to me that, in spite of my knowledge, the world might not turn out the way I wanted it to. My daughter was not supposed to grow up, overdose one night, and become a drug addict that I understood opened a delicate portal to lower forms allowing such things as "Electronic Mind Control," Alien Soul Wanna Be (human), or an Archon entry. I must have done something wrong, I kept thinking. I drove my mind further into very deep states of anxiety and depression.

How could I, for one minute, place such guilt on my lap? My journey is my journey with my Creator, and every step of the way has been a design in the magnificent thread of existence..~~ *There is nothing that has been placed before you by mistake. Every encounter has been designed to bring you to the level of awareness that you have now, to your current state of existence. There is no other way to unravel the essence of who you are except to have the human soul be placed in an atmosphere where one can play out the glory of one's own existence. One understands the glory of one's own existence by experiencing out of the mind, if you will, that of which is not of itself. You are literally creating your higher self by losing the lower self through trials and tribulations. The planet is in the process of recreating herself or rather ascending herself. All things will ascend. All planets are embryos that are turning into stars. You are the embryos of the Infinite Supreme realizing that you are turning into and awakening the star, or the higher supreme that we are. Do not forget your microcosmic and macrocosmic world; do not forget your inner world is indicative of your outer. As within for you, so is without, as within for the planet, so is without for the planet. Each person, as the col-lective consciousness, is waking up and hearing that there is a higher realm.*

One is restricted by the senses: Senses are your limitations, in your con-stricted reality, the senses of touch, taste, smell, and sight limit the percep-tions of the other realms of existence. In higher states of your consciousness you reach, you will see and understand all possibilities are playing out in other realms simultaneously. You understand these realms when you are taken out of yours. You are taken out of your realm through the breakdown of the ego and your ego is broken down when you wake from the dream of separation from Source. You wake from your dream of separation through your discoveries and experiences, you yourself, have brought yourself to very high subconscious levels to unravel what it is you need to bring your being to the star it is becoming. Yes, the highest supreme states of your being and the highest supreme states of the planet you are on do exist in this eternal moment of now.

In each given moment, ask for the lesson. Ask for the awakening in your soul to take its place so that you may no longer experience the unpleasant experience you perceive. Once your awakening takes place, you will no longer need that experience. Remember the experience that you are having is an experience that calls you to understand that you yourself are the brightest star with the world, the I' am. You will constantly call to yourself the experiences needed to understand that you, too, are Gods. Therefore guilt yourself not one bit. Guilt will keep you caught in the Matrix. It will keep you caught in the dream of separation from me. Once you realize your truth, set yourself free to go and sin/separate no more. Wisdom is everything you will ever need in this lifetime, and in acquiring wisdom, one must take a serious path. Nonetheless, it is a path one must take. Everyone must take this path.~~

PART TWO

FROM THE BIRTH FORWARD

CHAPTER 19

THE BIRTH

I watched my daughter bravely give birth to her beautiful precious serene son. Her eyes gazed up at the father with the unspoken words I heard her say… You and I are bringing life to world right now, this is it…It was the most magical moment I had ever seen two people share. She was so brave, so strong. The nurse lifted her son and placed this baby that she denied existed on her chest and she, in that moment, awoke…my daughter's illusion, my daughter's psychosis about not being pregnant was not there this minute her son laid on her belly. She lifted him with love and urgency and kissed and kissed and kissed him. It was real; life was real in that moment as if nothing was dysfunctional outside the delivery room. I wanted to stay there. I made sure I looked at everything intensely, calculating in my mind what everything looked like so I would never forget. We all cried with emotion. I could not believe how powerful she was, even the nurses commented on this. She was oddly powerful as if she did not feel pain. I was shocked that she did not feel pain, as if the reptilian portion of the brain took over. Nonetheless watching this life being born miraculously as nature took over and brought her son's body through her birth canal was a pure design of creation that put me in touch with the true reality of bringing life into this world. It was if the flower of her womb was budding open the head of a baby. It was exactly like the creation of a flower getting ready to bloom to life. Life was life and it was coming into existence before my very eyes! Life was life creating itself before me! I watched his body go from a guppy like state of flopping around as the doctor released him from my daughter's body, to purging the birthing fluid out of his mouth as he took his first breath, which brought the body to life. It was stunning!

I stood in the delivery room as a person in my daughter's life named Skye a friend that loved and cared about her. I did not stand in the delivery room as a mother. "You are not my mother, you are not my mother," I heard over and over. I had mixed feelings between wanting to support her and wanting to tear her apart for denying me the right that I earned to be a grandmother. I was exhausted. We were up all night. I had to sleep on the floor at the hospital. There was a caretaker there for Lara helping assist her with her needs. Lara had asked her to go in the delivery room with us. Lara held her hand during the delivery and made it a point to not hold mine. She had never met this woman.

That is the job of the Archon inside her. That is its exact job. To do its demon job and discredit my validity to its fullest in the deepest way possible. In the deepest way it could through my offspring(s). The Archon, "Taylor" made it a point to devalue me. I am the Light Worker staring at this Archon inside her in the face screaming through my energetic waves to get my daughter Lara. "There is a child here and you're in my way" The Archon then is prepared to go full force to "get Lara" **out of the picture.** If Lara were to come forth, the Archon cannot live and encompass a body. If the Archon were to step aside then Lara my daughter will have to come back. She would return and face her grim reality. The reality of leaving her life and her baby, her home, her ambitions. All while the Archon will feed more and more from the confusion and trauma it's creating.

I didn't know at the time it was the Archon(s), along with Mind Control Technology. I didn't know that my life was being ripped out of me at the core because the Archon Network had control. I didn't know that it was beaming down at me with laser beams of hell making sure it knew the deepest possible ways to curse. I stood there again with my gut staying silent so that I could not harm **her**. Worse yet I did not know how to protect myself against her attacks because I didn't feel I had permission. She was having a baby; she was in a mental institution; and she was highly medicated, she, she, she!

That's all I ever did was put my feelings aside because it never seemed appropriate. She was always in the middle of some crisis in front of them. There was no time to be concerned about me. This time I stopped caring about

The Birth

that. I don't know if it was Al-Anon or spirit although I am sure both. I decided to remove myself from another very difficult situation. It was difficult indeed.

I watched this life being born, and I watched my daughter hover over this baby as if it was the only thing she had. I was proud of her being protective of her son. I also understood her mind was distorted with the hormones that were controlling her body after the intensity of birth. She became angry with me when I stated I was his grandmother. The nurse asked her who she wanted to have a wristband to go in and see the baby in the nursery, and she purposely said I was not allowed. I stood and looked at him through the window for hours dreading what was going to happen next. I stood there and stood there. I asked to hold him. Somehow I was able to. I was in the hallway so I could be watched. I held him up and held him so tight. I looked at his bundled body and kissed his face over and over not knowing in that moment if he was going to be in my life or not. Not knowing if I could hold him being my newborn precious first grandson. Not knowing if I was holding him sending him out into another life.

CHAPTER 20
THE STATE TAKES THE BABY!

My daughter could not sign the birth certificate and use her real name. She would have signed it Taylor Brown. She was not Lara, and it was obvious. I knew what was going on behind the scenes. I felt that weird feeling a mother gets when she knows something is going on with her offspring. I did not want Children Services called. I wanted him safe as well as I did not want him in the system whatsoever. I had urgently asked the father to call months ahead of time over and over to understand the complications of what may be going on, but he chose not to. I did not want them involved.

Lara, whose mind and body was taken over, insisted I was not her mother and insisted the father was not the father. We had no chance. Child services took our baby and it has been a nightmare ever since. They and their system run under the dark Kabal showed up at the hospital bed and my life was to change again forever.

I fell to my knees in tears when I could not bring my grandson home as the father and I had arranged. I had no idea of what these people do. I stood for months on end with fuming resentments at the system and everyone who even walked through it. It has been beyond imaginable for me to conquer this resentment. I did my rituals, I prayed, I chanted, I saw my spiritual guide, I cried, I wrote…I could not shake my increasing suspicions about DCFS and what it really meant and my increasing suspicions of it all tying into the Kabal. I also could not shake the horrific cruelty as to how we treated each other as human beings. It was clear to me now that my gut and the Light Beings were vibrantly speaking to me and at every angle I turned.

THE STATE TAKES THE BABY!

At first it appeared as if everything was on the up and up. In the middle of the beginning of the court proceedings, the Judge had granted the father rights to his boy once the paternity test cleared. In fact that was all I ever was told in the beginning once they took my daughter's baby. They were just going to identify the father. I was told it was the only legal right they had to take the baby since there was no legal case of abuse in progress. Ross M, the social worker who came for the initial interview with us from DCFS, spoke to me. I recall it like it was yesterday. He stated that it didn't matter what the father had done in the past. They could not use past history to take a baby or child. It didn't matter what kind of crime the person had committed. I was on the floor shaking with reward and justification. I couldn't believe it after all we went through back and forth up to this point. We were finally granted the rights to our baby. He's the father, but Lara had denied he was to the social workers at DCFS, therefore a massive investigation of everything he was and was not took place. She continued denying me as her mother and was excessively protective of the only thing she had, her new baby.

I went out and got the rest of the things we needed for immediate needs and said a prayer standing over his crib in gratitude. I could not believe we were getting him. The next couple of days, as the paperwork was in progress, seemed so charged with emotion, and I was so excited. We, the father and I, drove down the morning we were scheduled to meet the foster parents at DCFS and reclaim our infant and bring him home to his family…I was so happy…I was so happy…

Things were to unfold as such: The judge had granted the father rights to his own child provided he do x, y, and z while the paperwork was in progress. Z was a drug test. My spirit started to drop down as if it were crumbling in my stomach, my solar plexus, my third emotional Chakra. The pieces came together when he did not show up for his appointment. Our baby is standing in the arms of the foster care parents outside DCFS, waiting for us to pull up and bring him home. Before we could grab him, we were taken in a room where we violently were told it was not going to happen. I was in shock. I could barely speak as there was this endless pit feeling in my stomach of terror. I drove home in a trance and once I got there I again violently fell to my knees with childlike pure tears screaming "God, why!"

A Light Worker named SKYE

The days went immediately forward where now the topic and the attention in the courtroom then turned to me as they were now looking at me to be the baby's caretaker while the parents were preparing themselves for meeting all court requirements. This is when **I** was faced with the court system myself and met so many people so very lost in the illusions of the world.

I hated the courtroom. I hated the smell and the symbolism. I hated the mentality. I wasn't nervous that I would not be able to connect with my grandson because of my medical marijuana use and my levels being so high the day I tested. The social worker had told me they were use to people on medical marijuana, it being legal here in California. It was all on the up and up. I had clearance from my primary doctor, and they knew that. I was in great stable condition. I felt great, nervous but of great mind. After what I went through the first time I had drug tested per the courts request, not being able to urinate having to stand in front of a stranger the odd way I was asked to with my shirt way up to my breast and my pants down to my knees, standing while the stranger took her up close and personal view making sure I wasn't swapping urine. After not being able to urinate in this unusual way, I was out and out told they were going to put me down as a missed test, therefore guilty (dirty test) is what they pretty much labeled me. You bet I was medicating. It relaxed me enough to urinate but of course with higher levels. It was almost another one of the weird things that seemed to have psychically kept me away from my grandson and my path with him.

It was the day after we supposedly were to show up and bring the baby home. I was a nervous wreck. He was packed and ready to come home to us and he couldn't. I medicated heavily to relax. It greatly helped my depression and of course I wasn't on any prescription pills. I also had never been in a position where I had to test for anything before like this so I was unaware that levels had anything to do with it. I probably wouldn't have tested like that, although I want to keep the cannabinoids (CBD) levels of the healing agent in the herbs high enough to maintain the extreme benefits it has brought me. I had an opportunity in court to express the benefits of my medical use of Cannabis to the judge this time; it was life changing for me. I was in major depression before Cannabis and my spiritual downloads. It changed my life and brought me back to being a productive active member of society. It helped get me out of bed in the morning and assisted in relieving me of major depression.

THE STATE TAKES THE BABY!

I was so thankful that for the first time in years I wasn't pumping pills down my throat just to sleep. It gave me that ability to work, not just get my ass out of bed, and it dearly desperately helped my right arm that I so longed to have back, damaged from repetitive stress injury, carpal tunnel syndrome and tennis elbow combined. I at one point had to learn to write with my left hand, my right hand giving me so much trouble and pain. I was making my living using my hands with my massage and skin care work, which I had been doing for years. Most of all, though, I was able to have a minute away from the mental pain I had over my daughter. I just wanted one minute not to feel the pain, just one minute not to have the thoughts of her merged with my brain coupled with anxiety. I longed for freedom. I found that when I found God or Creator God. Herb assists me in keeping my pressure low. I miraculously did not have that freedom with marijuana before my profound spiritual experience. Prior to my Kundalini experience, marijuana was like an acid trip to me. I hated it. Didn't use it. It wasn't until after I had a molecular structural change with my DNA upgrade that I was even able to comprehend herb and it's true spiritual and physical attributes.

It was nice she had given me a moment. I mean after all it was my Grandson. How kind of her to LET me speak! I was sworn in. I gave my explanations of my medical marijuana use as well as explained my current certification in herbology. I appreciated the time and honor she did give me. She also did acknowledge that it may be a substance that works for me and that I seemed like a reasonable and together woman. I have to say that felt very comforting.

The visitation, I could not fathom this. I couldn't believe the criteria and stance DCFS and the courts took on visitation. I, the grandmother, was only allowed one time a week for under an hour for our precious newborn that had just been brought into this world to hold. She then said she could not offer me the unmonitored visitation because she had to be fair to everyone, hence everyone else she told could not use marijuana and be with their child. She stated she would entertain the idea of having DCFS work something out with me for regular **monitored** visitation. That they were going to be ordered to do so or that it would state so on the orders to them. I did not like or understand or agree with her knowledge of marijuana and how it affected the body. I later clearly and vibrantly expressed this. I actually was ecstatic that Children Services was going to see me on the orders to try to work with me better on this visitation thing. I had worked so hard at getting respect over this. I felt like it was a victory because DCFS and the foster care agency had had to take me serious now. I was so sick of getting shoved aside. It was prayer and rituals that allowed me to calm down enough to send out a pure solid message to the universe that heard me.

I had plunged forward to rid myself of the heartache of having had my grandson taken over by some organization that I had such animosity toward while we waited for a solution only to turn around and astonishingly learn that the father was now incarcerated. I peeled over to calm the tightening in my stomach. I thought the pain would stop as I caught my breath, but it did not. My heart dropped and kept dropping. There was no chance now whatsoever to get our newborn. They were not releasing to me, the mother was in a facility, and the father was now incarnated for something in his past that happened to have caught up to him and NOW. I couldn't believe it, I was crushed, my heart was crushed, and I loved this baby. It was proud instinct to have him nurtured by his mothers scent and the closet he had thereafter my daughter was me. It was also so very unnatural what they were doing! And I had also secretly hoped that by Lara loving him it would heal her. I knew the magic of love. I could not get that kind of support from the system. They were so ill in getting any movement to have her see her son. They were consumed with fear that something would go wrong. Not one even attempted to get visitation for her but me. Not even the social worker or her guardian—the system was not concerned with her bonding with her newborn whatsoever. Perhaps the only word they heard was schizophrenia or mental illness and not one word after that. Although I had words after that. I saw how she was with the baby.

It was so interesting when I first wrote this book or first started interpreting this book. It was very clear to me that this was where I was to start learning about and applying the "crashing of the old paradigm"/ getting out of the Matrix and honoring the ridding of the EGOIC MIND, THE WORLD OF ILLUISONS. The exact kind of people I had been thrown into the mix with were people that were swimming in occultism. I was also increasingly learning and seeing the Archons all around this. I saw the illusions of our belief in separateness, the job of the Archons. I saw the people running to worship the courts in disillusionment, the job of the Archons, and I saw the dark energy of separation run the whole thing, the job of the Archons. I saw the Archons inside my daughter and I heard them reach over and touch the social workers and lawyers with holes in their being and darkness around their energy, and I was forced to hand over my grandson. I saw those Archons full force all over this, just like they are supposed to be.

Things just did not feel right to me. Not at all. Nowhere near right. They came in and took this four-day-old baby from the hospital. He had a loving safe crib to come home to with cloths and supplies, with love and security, with family, with safety. "What is going on," I would say to myself." I just couldn't shake this. Two separate workers had come to my home and gave me flying colors of approval as to the safety and protection this baby was to have. Why was there so much prevention to this baby that I just shared private moments with watching him being born and held at the hospital? Who are these people? I kept thinking as my gut was screaming!

I could not let any of this go, as I now believe I was not meant to let go of it at all. It became alarmingly clear to me later that I was interacting with the most profound darkest sinister corners of the US government that I ever even dreamed existed. It was I who had the awareness of what was really going on with their direct interactions with the occults and how I increasingly started to believe my grandson was a target for one of many dark purposes that these darker races running our planet use. Yes, that is what I said. Unless you are purvey to this information, of course, hearing this firsthand, it sounds quite preposterous, even to me, and I have a huge stretch in my imagination. In the dark and in the light, I will still think it's insane, that is until I review in my mind what I found out about our origins as human beings and all the vast array of things that came with it. And, of course, it was I that was going to be facing this huge battle alone as I surely was not going to be heard by anyone taking me seriously against a huge dark Kabal system. Nonetheless, I became trancelike and a fearless spiritual warrior who was not backing down. I visualized myself getting tortured, and I was not backing down. I am a Light Worker and that is a very tall order. I was placed here on purpose.

CHAPTER 21
LETTERS TO THE COURTS;
VISITATIONS *WARNING

As time went on I had more and more evidence to back my vibrant suspicions that was brought to my attention from the Light Beings. I couldn't shake what my gut was telling me. It would happen over and over and over. I would wake in the middle of the night as if I was being summoned from the command center from the galactic embassy. I started a series of letter writings to the original judge and everyone involved that progressively became stronger, entailing piece-by-piece detailed information on how our government was working with the darker Alien races. Races who worked with the Kabal, and Illuminati, who are in truth in control of all of the children in the "System." I also became aware we were not the only country that acted as such. It was in many countries around the world and so vibrantly present right here in Long Beach, California, where my grandson was in custody.

If I were to list every letter and every page you may not be done reading this book for a very long time and it would sound redundant. I wrote different letters at different times, although everyone involved got a courtesy copy. The main vital points were taken out of each separate one and listed below. I kept the topics together so you could follow portions of each letter without missing any crucial points. Two **asterisks** are given before each letter. In between the letters I continue on with my writings as I was writing and documenting life and how things were to play in and out along the way. The writings of daily life do not have two **asterisks** in front of them.

LETTERS TO THE COURTS; VISITATIONS...

If you recall I had shared with you the first portion of a letter that was sent to several judges at the Edmunds Children Family Courts here in Los Angeles. Here are the two proceeding paragraphs for a reminder and lead in. This will bring you back to the recognition of how it is all initially tied into child services.

*Warning: These letters are very graphic, if it is ever to much for your senses I suggest to pause and then go read the Enlightenment chapter to rebalance your energy.

Continuing on from here: ***A trait of the Illuminati is they always give us eloquent clues in plain sight. Hence tracing every major building in DC, winding into a perfect pentagram facing down. The White House also faces the star system Sirius A, where the Orion Council sits. Another eloquent clue, is a US judge sitting at a rectangular desk with other square shapes around them in a black robe specifically resembling leadership of the darker races over the planet. This is explained in detail in many of Michael Tsarion's seminars as well as other scholarly individuals.*

These reptilian/leaders of our country (behind the scenes) and the participants in the Judicial System from the darker side have their superior underground bases all over the planet, usually following grid lines and guarding our once holy star gates to other realms. There are some main ones now under New Berlin, with the Illuminati and their Controllers the Jesuits...

** At the center of this pentagram of course we find the "House of Templars" where of course our Freemasons created the Morals and Dogma codes, which are believed to be the origins of our procedures, which of course is a direct correlation to Lucifer. They refer to him as "Lucifer the light bearer, Lucifer the son of morning, it is he that bears the light." These locations also correspond with the grids/lay lines across the planet dominating our star gates and or earth vortex points. This of course we proved during the Gulf War when what was taken in Iraq (in this massive search of weapons of mass destruction) (which is under one of our star gates) (earth's Chakras a vortex point to other realms) was the artifacts from Sumeria that of course proves what I am telling you.

**The mode of operation, which our judicial system and government has been taught to run under, is to dominate and separate and control as in

DUALITY thinking, such as what our system does. You may come to under-stand through extensive research these procedures we see that came over from some of the survivors of the flood of Atlantis, the elites who used Lucifarian practices, who brought these forms of structures and practice to our civilization. Make no mistake, if you are involved with the system, you are involved with Luciferian acts that are clear to the **trained eye** -as we spot all over a courtroom and system the forms of hidden symbols and the laws portrayed, although it was not the full-blown Satanism that exists now. It was Luciferian and there is a difference. We are at what is shown to me and thousands like me that are also genetically coded to wake up and see that we are at the end of times and these ET races (predominately the Greys and Reptilians(insertion: some darker Pleadians and darker Zeta Retculi' fashions) along with our elites and presidents and Lucifer's descendents aka the well-known dark KABAL, believe they and the Illuminati are to take over our planet. You may understand this better in the Book of Revelations, although much of this book was taken apart and of course burned at the libraries of Alexandria.

**Some ET races (insertion: or sections of races) are good as we witness exchange of technology and we see that the higher races of the Zeta Reticules sections of the Raptoids, and some Pleadian races are communicating with us, even giving us our crop circle codes that are also about the changes that we are to prepare for. Other races are wanting to rule the planet with the elites and continue to run (and use) our government under the same mentality given to us from the Illuminati that have run our county and organizations alike for a very long time under what has been uncovered and we see proven and now known to be the Luciferian methods under the well-known dark Kabal.

Out of the blue this voice told me I had better check on Lara considering that it had been approximately nine months since she had been in this particu-lar program and I recall that the program she originally was scheduled for was approximately that amount of time. I suddenly called in a panic. In the time while I had taken the time away from the situation to nurture my soul there was another new social worker that had stepped in. It seemed okay since I had stepped back from the one she was working with over the last few months since Lara had her baby and things settled. I stepped back for reasons that were pure to me but often wondered what they had thought about me doing so. It bothered me that I thought about what other people at the facility thought of me not seeing her during that time. I guess it was because one time I had called her doctor to see how she was and she kind of nicely asked something to the effect of had I seen her myself for my own evaluation. I actually had wanted her opinion before I said mine. We had a great conversation but I had it in the back of my head she had asked me that, insinuating that if I wanted to know how my daughter was I could go and visit her myself. Now, the doctor did not give that tone whatsoever but for some reason I was sensitive. It felt like I was being irresponsible taking a break and taking care of myself. I even had to explain it to the social worker right away as if I had to apologize for doing something not so mother perfect and or make sure she knew what a great caring supermom I was by participating in Lara's life as much as I did. I felt I needed an excuse as to why I hadn't been there the times I wasn't. It was strange the things that went on in my mind that made me think I had to hurry up and prove what a great mom I was. Again it was this underlined feeling of not being a good enough mother, a delusion that I could somehow fix something I believe I gave her somehow, therefore me not being there to see her triggered something deep within me, but not necessarily real.

In the middle of our great conversation, the new social worker by chance in passing said "Oh, and I see her court date for her son is in two days." I was dumbfounded. Child services had not even informed me. It did not seem to faze me on one hand, but on the other it really irked me. Although at this point I had done so much work to get rid of my anger around this situation, I did not even want to go there. In fact I was unclear if I wanted to even go to court. I had stepped back from all the drama. I had loved it. I tossed my feelings back and forth adding in a new one here and there and taking out a few here and there. I also went to see my counselor and read him the very first letter I had written to the courts. In case I did indeed decide to go to court, I would have had some emotional support and understanding in the background.

I know that when going to my daughter's facility to see her I am faced with my daughter denying me being her mother, repeatedly. I haven't seen her in a while and had secretly hoped it would go away. I also absolutely knew if I did see her prior to some of my own healing over this whole baby situation coupled with I am not your mother psychosis statements that I would have treated her with anger that I was not going to be able to control.

A Light Worker named SKYE

In this time that I took for myself, I was able to bathe in some of the promises the Al-Anon program offers. The gift of freedom seemed impossible and also like something I wanted to protect forever. If I see her, is my freedom going to be taken away? I ask myself. I think if I had no tools such as things like I could walk away if I needed to, or don't take things personal, or hate the disease and the Archons in her and not her, then I couldn't go. I also believe if these two parents were not working on themselves like they were I would have not for one minute shown up in a dark, dense courtroom fighting a system I found horribly dysfunctional wanting to bring home a baby that I had to face could possibly have a better life with another family. However, I also didn't trust the system with babies. **Not one god damn bit!** I had to weigh everything. Do I want to see the judge after the letters I wrote, baring my heart? I would ask myself. It felt so vulnerable. I also felt so powerful. I stood by every feeling I had about them and dealt with it in the most honest respectable way I could by writing my letter(s). My letters were vibrant, not always respectable. Although, I made sure I was taken care of by myself the best I could, when I could. I did what I could to release and be honest. The rest I have and do realize I am powerless over. I am okay with that. Most of the time, and when I am not, I just believe its Creator God working through me to change what I can.

**The procedures that have grossly taken place in our country and in our court systems, which have people thinking they can take control and MISUSE POWER has dominated and sadly maneuvered its way into organizations such as Children Services and Children's Court. Most people are operating under a system that is carefully designed and controlled as the Kabal and Elites have brilliantly kept most in a subconscious trance, this deliberate psycho-tronic weaponry is mainly done through television, and structures exactly like this, this psychic warfare that is so highly evolved and highly effective. Hitler was involved with these ET (Alien) races. He was a master of mind control, very much like what is going on now. Unless you have been taken outside of the hologram that is so brilliantly portrayed, and placed outside the Matrix, make no mistake you will remain under such mind control. Although some I see like this and shall remain in the trance although not much longer with the changes to come.

** These Alien lower races combined with the dark Kabal Illuminati members, which we believe exist among the courts, use the social workers like

*puppets to do their paperwork. In the meantime our elites that own our banking system (Federal Reserve, which really isn't even ours as we are owed by the British) coupled with parts of our government **(not all)** that work with these dark entities live off fear. They literally suck on our terrifying emotions. Our terror is their breath and that is literally how they take their breath. They create wars and chaos to create control afterward and dominate, exactly what the courts do. Make no mistake. We see they created the major wars we have experienced as well as 9/11 as well as much proof now has come forth about Japan and now Hurricane Isaac as we see these people are involved in HAARP. They believe they own this planet. They create the highest grossed acts possible to promote the best fear possible to feed their Dark Lord. These are done during their rituals when a baby boy is born between September and November like my new grandson was born, and they are used for the sacrificial rituals that I have been shown exist, although I believe they no longer use the Vatican for the rituals, as too many Light Workers found out. As you will come to understand many things happen on the Earth's dragon grid lines, the thirtieth and thirty-third meridians of the earth, where some of our elite banking system lie, as well as Masonic temples, the JFK assignation, top world churches, top world events, wars, and tragedies. These are put at the cross points where the dark vampiristic energy feeds. May you also understand this is how we see people in the court system now and what you must face as how you are being viewed.*

Because my grandson was born of a mentally ill mother, I'm not sure he would qualify for these sacrificial rituals. They only choose babies of fresh pure blood (preferably Israel Lights because Satan believes it's the purest blood apparently.) My grandson may have infant blood for them to drink but they would not want the blood of a mentally ill mother. They literally have to drink their blood. Although as it is morbidly gross to even discuss, it is imperative to protect all children and face reality. Although it should concern your courtrooms that if you are to transfer or sell off a baby or take a baby from a home or transport a baby (newborn especially) in any way shape or manner such as during September to November each year when these rituals are performed then you are potentially giving that baby forth for sacrificial rituals that are happening and especially now since we are at the end of times (time meaning linear) and there is a desperate need to give their darker lords their food, so to speak.

A Light Worker named SKYE

Also here in California, Long Beach California. Long Beach is very well known for the darker forces and the Illuminati involvement with children, and of course we all know they literally run children services courts. They are in control of any court system you see; **there is no separation between Satan and a courtroom, they are literally feeding off each other. If you understand a man named Jay Parker and his teachings you will understand his history being abused by the people that our judicial system takes orders from, the Illuminati, the dark Kabal, the people who literally are in control of the babies you take away from our homes. He was one of the children who made it out of the occult and talks about the damage done to him and how much of the practices and meetings are out of Long Beach. He will not be the only one with this information. He is just one that survived. There are thousands now. He is also one of the many educated people who know what the United States is involved in when they take children. There are more and more profound whistleblowers going to be coming forward, I promise. I have had no media contact, meaning I am not fed food from the poison that the Illuminati feed the masses. I was asked to omit all forms of news from my consciousness three years ago (insertion: at the time) so that the pure information from the light would reach the planet. The whistleblowers that are authentic correlate with the information given from the Light Beings. **They are going to tell you what I have been screaming at the courts over since a case had started over my grandson that ignited my attention to such an alarming degree. Baby Trafficking, US Rituals, October, Long Beach, California,** and all the changes that will be taking place on the planet. The more I screamed the more they tried to arrest me and shut me up, and pin me a crazy fanatic woman, another Illuminati trait by the way. They always make the other person as agitated as possible, enough so that their natural human reaction to their occultism makes that person seem insubordinate or crazy. Most people are so controlled by them subconsciously, they don't even question the laws that walk themselves right smack into mind control.*

The Queen of England, who represents one of the bloodlines, hence being part of the Reptilian Gray (and or the Astro Alba's who created the Grey's in general) race has been arrested (silent arrest) for trafficking children from Philadelphia, another huge Illuminati base where they take children from the United States besides from here in Long Beach as equally well known is Pasadena.(see Kenneth. Annette.)

Santos Bacconi a brilliant Astrotheologist and well respected speaker and researcher on the Occults taking children from our Government:

Quote (word per word): "They get a bounty I think they get about A HUNDRED THOUSAND POUNDS every time these common purpose guys come knocking on your door stating a neighbor has reported to us there is some trouble with your child and we need to ask your child some questions cause were going to steal them from you because you're not fit. Then they right up all their reports about you and they take your children. Then they take their children from their parents. This is how sick they are/half those children get eaten for blood sacrifices. They do the most ungodly things I would dare not say." March 2013

The Vatican and its corporate infrastructure, hence the banking system and elites that are running this planet have their home base in Switzerland, as explained by one of the many through George Kavassalis (in the endless teaching and education he has given us having had such contact with the dark and being abducted only to break out of the Matrix) as you will understand they, are as a whole, one Unit, the Vatican and the US banking structure. They are making their plans for depopulation and to have dominance over this world and it goes in many layers as they are running the planet interdimensionally and off world in many different ways. One way is with their Dark Lord pronounced VatiKanna hence "Vatican." This is where they perform their rituals, on the thirty-third dragon grid line of the planet. Stuart Swerdlow, who educated us on the Montauk project, has explained the following very well. These procedures are correct in the ritual sense. This Dark Lord guarded the Swiss Illuminati during the war. Once the Dark Lord is fed through their sacrificial rituals of taking newborn baby boys born predominately in October through December (thoroughly explain the occult reasoning by Michael Tsarion and Stuart Swerdlow) by drinking the newborns' blood or DNA after the Dark Lord has entered the vessel through sexual rituals of the root Chakra (also explained in Robert Stanley's book Washington D.C. a portal for the Gray Reptilians). Once the blood is consumed, *the DNA coding from the Dark Lord is now in the person who drank the blood, enabling them to receive strategic information about advance sciences, propulsions, technology, and military strategy moves in war. The newborns that are transported throughout the United States are part of their rituals. Besides, for the Vatican, many rituals consisting of pedophilia acts are done in Rose Valley Pennsylvania, Arden, Delaware, and Medford Lake, and Riverton. It is a superior sophisticated program far greater than the human eye can catch and literally run by Satan and his master planners. Jay Parker explains there are 800,000 missing children in the United States. We as a whole understand many of them are taken by the gray reptilian races that are shape shifters that pose as people. May you understand when your Chakra centers are invaded one will be controlled where, when, and how to meet and how to handle the infant, that means all through the court proceeding. (insertion: It is also well known now many our judges are under this mind control). There are many reports of President Bush Senior shape shifting. He basically says to the people who have seen this, "Go ahead tell everyone what you see. No one would ever believe you." He was right, that's why they get away with it.*

**Children Services came in and took my four-day-old grandson from the hospital and started their proceeding to have him be one of the thousands in line for their pedophilia and sacrificial rituals and I sat there and watched each of the workers and the lawyers and the judge walk right into their dark Kabal trap.

During the next courtroom proceedings concerning the baby's fate, the lawyer from Children's Services actually asked the judge if I could be omitted from the courtroom all together and not even sit in there to listen to what they were going to do to him. This was when the father was incarcerated and the mother was hospitalized and when I was being withheld from him. That's when my suspicions were screaming at me and my anger and my terror. What are they trying to do to this baby? Why are we all being withheld from him? Mysteriously they did not want me in that courtroom and said it was due to my aggravation and my treatment toward the staff. Not only did I stay in the courtroom, I walked out with double the visitation hours than what I was entitled to. We actually live in a world where Children Services go out of their way to keep a family apart, the social worker and their team had it set up for me to only visit with my grandbaby two times a month; a grandparent is suppose to get a whopping four. They said they didn't have room for me to have my other two days. They mailed me letters instead of calling. It blew my mind that they could take our babies from us and then not even give us our right to visit them. They conveniently did not have space for me. I had to beg for two hours a whole month, and this was not all right with me. That was a tiny baby that needed to be held and nurtured by his family. He was being looked at and visited by lawyers and strangers instead that saw him more than his family. The heart, the human voice and the touch for life didn't matter, and it was burning me up inside. I went to bold lengths letting everyone know how I felt about their views. I was very persistent in my drive to let everyone know of the light of the world and the karma they were going to get. They tried very hard to exit me out of the picture. The karma I always mean as our oneness, the law of cause and effect. It seemed inaccurate to me the way these people judge character; it seemed inaccurate to me to have a court system so lost in their own whirl of laws and procedures they were forgetting there was a baby here that had a family that loved him.

The doctor had okayed the visits and said my daughter should be capable and fine for a visit. The father and I already brought him once on the father's visit. Lara did great. There were people always around and it is a monitored situation, and that is exactly what we needed for his safety. Why isn't this being arranged? Nothing. I got nothing from them. Again Children Services ignored my calls. There was a dead end everywhere I turned.

*** Since your grandson is a white- skinned baby boy born in October during the annual ritual time and the baby is in Long Beach, California, where several of the Illuminati members are located for the actual transfer(s), and since you are aware of this, the lawyer will be asking you to leave the courtroom. In the meantime if you keep calling the agents with such unprecedented concerns, we will arrest you and keep your infant away from you for interfering with such trafficking plans. Although before you visit, you and your family members are going to have a series of scans. We are going to tell everyone that checking backgrounds are for your grandson's safety, and they will not know they are completely fooled. Of course this was a tactic used by the exact same Alien races that you all work with now that were working through and with Hitler to literally have people follow the dark,* *brilliantly and unknowingly. That way, once scanned we will have tabs on everyone of you for the sole purpose of the NEW WORLD ORDER. That's all that's in play for. It's so fun watching everyone believe it's for their safety. Records mean nothing to us and they are easily changeable through the Archons, but we will have everyone all do massive paperwork as a decoy, posing as a tangible reason to have you parents labeled insufficient. As the masses are fooled we'll continue to keep your grandson. Our continued plans are to give him a set of vaccines installed by the dark Kabal for tracking purposes as well as forms of mind control, and to make sure his spiritual gland will be calcified from the truth.*

Then if you're one of the lucky ones whose child is not taken over by Satan and his descendents working through DCFS, then we will keep your baby on this probation period for six months in case there are not enough children found. In case the war starts and we'll need more blood from newborns to get our strategic information, we will have social workers prepared to set up lies to the courts by their lawyer's working through the Leeches on the human aura convincing everyone the family members who are trying to protect your grandson from the real criminals should be kept away.

**I was referring to myself here: Ms. LA to show our power, we always use child human beings as collateral. Since you have your Akashic memory back, you may recall the exchange of humans held in reserve for the genetic manipulation with these darker Alien races that we sent these humans and children to. Now Ms. LA. if you have a better plan for this newborn baby, we are going to continue to make sure we keep you away from him. We have made this clear. Our social workers are very trained under the dark Kabal's orders. Surely though, I am starting to think Ms. LA it might be time for a physiological test before you do see your grandson. Don't you understand you're the only one on the planet with this exact sci-fi story. All those people mentioned. Well they are not real. They don't exist. The scriptures written throughout history in many different cultures was all for airy fairy people who couldn't make it in business. Those lines that trace the pentagram to each of our major White House buildings, come on, surely can't you see one of those lines must be CrOoKed. The Gray Alien theory, all the scientists, government officials, whistleblowers, presidents, citizens, Light

LETTERS TO THE COURTS; VISITATIONS...

Workers, contactees, are surely part of having high levels marijuana in your system. The Archons and Leeches, now the Gnostic and the Essenes wrote that for fun. They went out of their way to have some of the dead sea scrolls burned in the Library's of Alexandria for no reason. Those aliens and the one Annunaki Brother doesn't work with our US government under New Berlin. They didn't work with Hitler before. He didn't do much so don't worry about your grandson. Light Workers, ETs, and Angels were never mentioned in the Sumerian Text. The rituals and Archons. Oh please, there are not excessive killings of children around those ritual months. That is not the documented way those rituals are reported. There are no document reports of the largest Illuminati connections in Long Beach, California. Children's courts have nothing to do with government whatsoever at Long Beach DCFS. Children Services doesn't have to follow the Law aka the dark occults. They are a separate unit, and they are not under the Jesuits Orders. There are no thirty-third dragon lines where the most horrific crimes happen. There is no reason a government would be in need of strategic plans for war. There is no occult reasons why the major issues are over or around the star gates such as Iraq or the Gaza Strip. There was no disclosure project May 2013 by our well respected Light Worker Robert Doylan. That must have been a fantasy of yours too. None of this correlates with children and the law. Yes, Ms. LA, you should take that psychological test; we want you to register sane in an insane society. Ms. LA while you're sitting way in the back pew to justify my hierarchy and support my symbolism, we are going to come in to rip your heart out. Any questions? Maybe you should think twice about your marijuana use. Can't believe you'd give up your kids for drugs. It's you who has chosen to use marijuana and have a misdemeanor on record for aggressive driving, therefore entitling you unfit. Why are you blaming me...Ms. LA?

Lara looked utterly beautiful today in court. Her beautiful soft golden hair had grown so fast since I had seen her, it had a crystal shine to its goldenness as it laid across her porcelain clear skin. I could not stop staring at her fresh skin and hair. It used to terrify me to know what I know about the body and how it operates and how precious and delicate her body was to see her meth skin and stringy hair against her frail body as I flash up a memory. Today was so refreshing. I couldn't stop looking at her. I also couldn't believe how clear she was. Her mind has cleared up a lot. Her social worker was right. It was somewhat of an aha moment of "Wow my daughter is coming back to herself."

My daughter, the girl before the drugs and the Archons, that daughter, my daughter, was the girl I was visiting as we hung out in the morning hours before we were called in. We walked around, ate out on the patio, went outdoors a few times so she could smoke, watch some thing on my iPhone, laughed, and had a great morning. During the court proceedings inside there was not much we could do, considering the father had not been able to be there because of his incarceration. The judge had scheduled an order for a couple months from now for him to show up in hopes that the courts would release him to his hearing, which was what I thought was happening this time although it did not.

I have had to let go of any idea of how I think things should play out with this baby. What I have done is reset the Universe within me affecting the outer Universe sending it the energy from within me that is pure of heart. It can be read across any distance to anyone anywhere on any planet, knowing that we are microcosmic and macrocosmic, and that "I am that I am," claims my right to claim.

What that means is I cannot control others direction or outcome or disease and I also realize I have no limitations in Creation as to how I would like my own experience to be so therefore the only thing for me to do is hold the profound energy space of the "feelings" I would feel from the love I feel when I am with my grandson. I feel the warmth of his love. I picture him here with me on my deck and where I have visualized him with me while I hold him overlooking the mountains, and what the "feeling" would feel like. It is the "feeling" that we send out to the Universe letting it know what we want more of. Those surroundings and those feelings will be what enters my realm and becomes manifested. I carry this amazing energy around with me and that is what I send out to the Universe to send back to me, we are co-Creators. I also send out the vibration of seeing my daughter here holding her son with her long red hair and porcelain skin both hugging and kissing me goodbye as they go about their day, and what that would feel like and how it warmed my heart. I hold that space in my heart of experiencing that energy within my life, the energy before the experience, and how we draw it into life **first.**

The Universe hears my heart and will set out to allow me to experience what it is I am sending out and when, my good is never withheld from me. We may have an illusion of separation from this dimension to the next but we are never without in true reality. There is no separation between me my Creator and the world I create; it is a coordinated whole between me, the Divine energy, and the Cosmos.

**I called endlessly screaming, "There is an infant in a crib growing day by day while you are not returning my calls. Why no visitation?" I screamed to the supervisor. "Why are you not sending this baby to his parents to hold?" And, if not them then why is he not being held by his immediate family. "He must have touch. You must touch a newborn!" I screamed. This is Family Services and any health care professional and psychologist will tell you this is imperative for his immediate health. I, we, held him forever in the hospital so he would know his family. We must hold him. This is a sacred newborn for God's sake. "Why can't I hold him?" While his mother remains hospitalized and the father was incarcerated, I was on the sidelines deliberately being held back and prevented from seeing and visiting my first newborn grandson, precisely so they could prepare his trafficking plans. Mysteriously enough I was tipped off twice that my precious grandson was up on a website to sell white-skinned baby boys. All the while the crib at my house we had prepared for him remained standing and empty. I screamed with endless calls. The mystery continues when I received a generic letter from Alexis A. stating the foster care agency would no longer work with me. She had zero explanation other than my interactions with the staff and my grandson. I again begged for an explanation as to specifics stating "I have everything on video, what is possibly going on that you see suitable to cancel my visits, I expressed?" To this day not one person has an explanation as to what I actually did that would constitute taking a baby away from the grandmother and preventing visitation.(insertion" after the first initial set of visits).

**My poor grandson laid in his crib alone without his family and spent it with a temporary mother. His pure loving family members sat home and his presents were dropped off to him on January 10.

I am not too enthused about seeing the social workers from Children Services. I am, even if delusional, enthused about having a chance for them to correct a wrong they made about me during the Christmas situation. I prayed and demanded justification so hard from the universe, so hard that this would not go unnoticed. I cannot believe they are ordered to get a hold of me and work things out. I want them to fess up to their lie. I want them to face that because of the disregard for me and their dishonesty that they ruined a grandmother's precious holiday celebration with her first newborn grandson and they had to live with that fact the rest of their lives and all because of policy and paperwork. I had done so much work with the universe I had known that I knew the law of cause and effect. I knew without a doubt the consequences one had to face when they crossed the law of universal oneness. I can feel myself wanting to tear them apart with how dare you lectures and how rotten they are. I do, but the more I do and I did the more my shoulders tensed and my hands started to burn as I rubbed them together faster and faster the harder and harder I think until I am shaking and sweating stewing over how right I am…but it is **my** body that is shaking and **my** body that is stewing and **my** body that is sweating as the lower energies of the world feed the anger I put out into it. I put out love in the world. The cosmos feels love. I put out hate and anger, and the vultures of the lower natures feed off it. It literally keeps dense matter on the earth. I don't want to do this. I can feel the crappy feelings I have. Of course, that is the tool for healing although stewing in this like I have almost creates dark energy around me starting in the form of tight shoulders and tension. I watch myself notice this, as watching myself is my tool knowing that I am caught back up in the third dimensional word of duality and the right or wrong old paradigm thinking. I don't want to get to far into that world and then carry the dense matter of tension on my shoulders; it will keep eating at my body. I stop there, clear my mind, and then clear my body not letting it fester into something further. I relax as I do some yoga moves preparing for my evening bath. I am going to unwind. I am going to consciously trust. I feel guided. I feel the higher spirits have everything lined up for me and everything lined up for my grandbaby and for some reason I trust it. I feel peace around the higher purposes knowing they have clearly directed me. It might be a direction I don't want right now, caught in the moment like not having our baby here now, but it is a direction for the bigger purpose that is for sure. I am not going to question this one more minute.

**They took time from me time is not something you take back. Interesting they took time, time is Saturn, Saturn is the female Lucifer.*

I am getting ready to visit the baby in about an hour. It will be the first time I am going to see him in a month and a half. The courts had me make arrangements with an outside caregiver, not the foster care agency. I had had videos of each month consecutively except this one. There was arguing between me and the courts just to get the right to visit him like this. Prior to my fight I was only seeing him two hours a month, and this is what I was so charged about. They call this family services and it is everything I experience but that. The only thing the courts represent to me is people that are tearing families apart.

The visit with my grandson was held at a park in Carson. He was adorable, oh my God. He was like God himself just brimming with innocence and authenticity. I watched him watch people while I held him and stared into his bright blue eyes visualizing to myself what it is like to come from spirit again and have the DMT release that one has at birth and death. I could tell he still had his. It starts to diminish when we all fall into the trance of the third dimension reality where separation and duality dominate and we are easily drifted off into the trance; until death.

I loved watching him. I secretly put my mind inside of his. It was like he was fascinated watching people. I held him and kissed him so much. It was such a joy. I asked if I could push him in the stroller, and it was a gift pushing him in the stroller. I don't know why that was the one thing I wanted to do with him that seemed normal but it was. We all take for granted the little things. Do you know how many times I would see a parent strolling their baby and that is all I wanted to do was stroll my grandson. It was as if strolling him was all there was in life, a simple thing I had to beg for.

My joy never seems to sustain itself when the "System" is involved. The visit wasn't supposed to even happen, apparently the social worker had again faulted on paperwork where it was not arranged in some appropriate manner. It again made me crazy. This time it made me so crazy, I gave her a phone call and told her I was going to follow her and one day we were going to have a talk. Afterward I thought to myself why would I want to follow this woman? I can't stand her and wasting my time following someone I can't stand was insane. So I started to triple my Al-Anon meetings, I visualized terrorizing this woman and those people every day. I was ripping with anger at all the frustration I had to go through seeing my first grandson and how every precious moment was robbed from me by the system, the system that I thought I was getting help from. I am not sure what made me think I was going to get something rational from an organization that is built on nothing but the irrational. In fact I had been abused so badly by the system for so long it was time to do what I could. Also, in fact it wasn't me that was so unjustly treated by a huge cutthroat system that could care less about mankind, it was now turning into nations.

One day in the middle of my chants, I told the Universal Mother light that I had done everything asked of my higher self and to relieve me of my anger about Children's Services and the foster care agency blocking my visitations with my grandbaby and the anger is still vibrantly here. I can't take it. I have to drive down and see this woman in person I told myself. How dare the foster care agency write down on their reports they were not willing to work with me and nothing happened. Although I had always believed that if you come in and take our children out of our homes you should probably roll out the red carpet. It showed in my words too. Nonetheless I knew that if I did not go I would be disrespecting my spirit and with all the work spirit has done with me there was no way I was going to ignore its voice now.

The Mother Light Being gave me clear directions to go do the project I was doing over here in my neighborhood raising the energy of the planet and preparing our minds and bodies through a designed yoga treatment I created. I did, and it was wonderful to release this anger over here in the mountains connecting with nature as I worked out and walked out my anger thinking about what I was going to say before I got there. The light instructed me to at least walk off my anger until 10:00 a.m. before I drove down and expressed myself, and if I waited then it would be a clear path to go. I did exactly as directed. When I was finished the need to go was gone. The next day the whole thing started again and I was directed from the light that it would be okay to go if I so chose. I was to express myself but also just be willing to let her know that I cared about how I personally affected people on our planet, and I did not want anyone walking around in pain or frustration over something I caused through my unkind words. I agreed to the terms exactly as directed. What I also knew is that me expressing myself these days is quite animated and I was going to hold nothing back and I wasn't kidding. I wanted my point made. I had actually prepared jail clothes just in case I was being prevented from saying what I needed to and being asked to leave before I was ready.

A month ago, out of the blue, I had recalled that I contacted the regional manager at the Foster Care agency and just happened to get hold of one of the main directors on accidental, purpose. I explained the situation to him as he took the time to listen. I continued to follow up loosely noticing he would connect with me upon returning to the office shortly after dealing with his father's illness. When we hung up the phone I got a clear message from spirit that his father was indeed making his transition and I sent them both light. I also received confirmation from spirit several times that I would be meeting him in person even though I felt this was going to be ignored all together. I secretly felt hurt though because I felt my needs were to be set aside because of his loss and I was not going to ever get this settled. Once he is back in the office I feared that compared to "the after the death of a loved one" my noise might not seem so important. I didn't want to bug him any further so I took direction from the Light Beings and drove myself down to Carson and walked in person myself and confronted what had been eating at me for months.

I walked in asking for Noel the foster agency manger who I had had the major problems with. She came out and alarmingly looked me in the eyes as I handed her the form sent to me from Children's Services stating their agency would no longer be facilitating my visits because of my interactions with my grandson and how I treat the staff. One by one I said to her what does this exactly mean, exactly what does mean, why did you do this to me and my family, etc., etc. That very second the Regional Manager out of nowhere walks through the door. I had never met him. I secretly knew he was going to be there. I'd had a vision of it, I saw it, I immediately said, "Oh yes, Mr. Wasson. My God you're hear. My Angels (I couldn't call them Light Beings, not many understand that) told me you would be here." He kindly let me in for us to immediately all sit down and hash this out. It couldn't have been a better moment designed by the universe all the way around. There was also no one in the office and it's usually packed with workers, interns, children, and families.

We sat for two hours and hashed out the paperwork word for word. There was nothing that constituted cancelling those visits like they did. There was correction needed but nothing to cancel visits. That man apologized to me on behalf of the company easily seeing there was confusion on the way things were handled and understood my genuine charge behind my emotions. He also stated that they had just had to get a restraining order on someone and were operating out of fear and tension. I am sure I didn't help much. I hated my grandson being in that system and it showed. All the while the manager had listened and corrected herself where needed. This invited me to do as directed from the Mother Light and correct where I was wrong and I did. I was saddened that my anger had affected another person on the planet the way it did and it was time for me to stop punishing everyone in my path for the position **I** was in. Even though I hated their action, I knew it was still my side of the street that I was responsible for.

I was then told that there would be a discussion with child services to reinstate my visits. Child services did not acknowledge this. I never heard a word, no calls returned. As stated, I was sent a letter from child services *not a phone* call indicating the two days I was to see him at DCFS, not the foster care agency.

**I know and you all know Children Services are absolutely available for more than two hours an entire month for a brand new baby for over four consecutive months. A professional baby swapping place definitely has hours available; the Illuminati do not run neglectful operations when matters of children are at stake.

Also, of which, when the worker usually arrived for the few visit I did get, she arrived fifteen minutes late. She said the remaining forty-five minutes would be in another room since my time had already started in the waiting room.

**Although another mystery sets in concerning this baby snatching scheme. Once the professional court-appointed monitor arrived, she blatantly said it was the most confusing operation she had ever seen and something very strange was going on there. She stated she had worked with courts and Children Services for a long time and she had never seen anything like this. Oddly and mysteriously we were not able to use her anymore and that the one visit we had never was supposed to even happen is what I was told. Oddly and mysteriously from that point on Children Services changed the social workers on the case all together and refuse to tell me why, or what happened. I didn't even get a letter two weeks late to the wrong address. Nothing and no explanation whatsoever. To this day my family and the community has no idea why they banned my visits, other than baby trafficking. I wrote continued letters about this to the Judge and the Illuminati involvement with the Long Beach Children's department. Why was she, the Judge, then removed from this case?

LETTERS TO THE COURTS; VISITATIONS...

It has been a few months now since I have seen my daughter. I had to just stop. Stop everything, stop chasing the baby, stop seeing her, and stop running around like a chicken with my head cut off and stop. Lara was suddenly and quickly and alarmingly back into the illusion that I was not her mother. It was after I sat with her right after Christmas after getting my heart broken having the baby's first Christmas visit/Christmas party terminated for us, only for her to tell me she gave away all the presents I had given her and that I am not her mom. I just left, kindly. I will never forget that powerful feeling of how denied I felt. My silent comment of exiting kindly sent probably more of an energetic message then all the babbling I did to try to change her throughout her life. It was the beginning of the end for me.

I had to stop. Nothing was working, and I was running into brick walls and had to surrender. I had to come to terms with the fact that this baby really may have a much better life away from all this mess. It felt so humiliating to hear myself say that. It felt like I was the matriarchal failure, I had my daughter in the mental hospital and my grandson in foster care, and I apparently was not living up to the standards that would release him to me according to the system—it was insane. It was the face of the Archon. Part by part, the eyes were Lara's denial toward me, it's mouth was having the baby being held from me, its nose was the evil in the system and it reeked of it. It literally had its own face and its own dark colors. It was an invasion from darker forces through the ethereal and it was beaming down at my light. That's what the Archons do. When a person wakes up and becomes more spiritual they will fight that, this is well known, the Gnostics call it the Demiurge as I mentioned in the Archon chapter, (also explained eloquently by Laura Magdalene); so much so you actually have to almost prove why you think you're so spiritual. It's like you have to put it in action, not just believe it just because your heart feels warm. You have to know it, experience its knowingness.

I saw myself engaging with the Archon. I interacted with it every day with my fuming anger. I feed its breakfast so many mornings. It was in the morning they said hello to me. The moment the brain starts before the morning chants. I saw myself trying to make insane people in the system sane and I was suffering from the craziness. I had to step back. I stopped calling social services and the foster care agency and I stopped seeing Lara. I started to feel more and more anger toward her that she was in this position and how it affected me and my relations to my grandson. I started to get so sick of the "I AM NOT YOUR MOTHER" scenario play out in my daughter's world. I was just so tired of getting emotionally abused and having my own profound set of emotions set aside because of how terribly sick my daughter was. Her being sick always made my feelings become second best because there was always an emergency at hand that took over any feelings I may have had. There was always the set of "how things should be" that I had to follow when it came to my feelings. She was sick, I was her mother, therefore it "should" be this way—my feelings should be set aside, I am the strong mother, she is the sick child, I kept thinking.

That had to stop, really, that had to stop. I had to stop feeding the madness and the Archons. It was so hard for me to grasp that it was my journey not hers. I had to hurry and fix how she was feeling before I could pay attention to my feelings. I will tell you that is one of the beautiful lessons from the light of the light. *~~For through you and your experience is my way for me to express the fullness of you, therefore you MUST take care of yourself first before anyone, even your child. For your child has a built-in instinct in her DNA that is too creating and realizing the God Self that she is becoming. She cannot do it through you or any-one. This "God Self" has to come from her and only her just as your awakening had to come through you, so please stand back my child of light, for you are all embryos creating the magnificent god versions of yourself. You have chosen to use this exact experience as your awakening. You came here to have this experi-ence with this soul called your child so that it would reawaken within you what you had all left before the fall!~~*What is the fall I ask?*~~The separation from knowing of our grandness and our oneness together, my offspring. This is your time to reunite and rejoin with me. Your child has led you here, bless her every move and allow yourself to carry on with the business of yourself.~~*

It was hard, it was odd, and it was unfamiliar for me to let myself have a life without worrying about my girl. It felt like if I had given myself permission to live and make something of myself while she was ill then I was abandoning her. This was not a healthy feeling I knew my Creator wanted me to have, as it was not my job to fix her anyway. I thank the Spirit for that too. If it really was my job to fix **her** it would have been done by now and/or we both may have been led further astray, it is her journey.

I have so enjoyed the last couple of months focusing on nothing but my life and what I want out of my life. The air has been fresh for me these days as I have plunged into my own character defects for some needed healing. I quickly made sure any nuisance like a character trait that would at all get in the way of my newfound freedom. I went to extra meetings, I wrote a lot, taught yoga, caught up on school, caught up with friends, went to the outdoor yoga sessions at Runyon Canyon in the park to learn, bonded with my plants and the little garden I was creating, and I have loved it. I started to do everything I ever wanted to do as if she never got sick. It felt so good, and I don't ever want to stop giving myself my life like this.

I found the break was the best thing I did, and I stayed back just enough to catch my breath and rekindle my heart. The heart, the spirit, the place where the Archon can't enter, the spirit, a spirited body, a body full of spirit. I was free emotionally so it was okay for me to be excited to see my daughter. There was a part of me that missed her.

During the court proceedings I had made it clear to the light that I would give the judge permission to enter my energy field any time she wanted to observe who I was. She actually had visited me in the astral saying hello on two separate occasions. I had immediately liked her energy. It was a strange unspoken thing. The stranger thing is I relived that astral trip over and over in my mind as if I had walked by her in the courtroom and actually lived it. In fact, the day before this hearing, I had several visions of seeing her outside the courtroom, as in passing by. I couldn't get it out of my head. I thought it was going to be in the elevator in close quarters, so that morning I woke extra early so I could go by the aroma-therapy section at Whole Foods since they open before court. It was like I was being pulled to be remembered by her energetically and subconsciously through the smells that would be the same smells of me during my visitations with her in the astral. I always use a smell like soothing aromatherapy. Smell is something the mind recalls the strongest out of all our senses. The olfactory system will bring us back to a memory faster than any other sense. When I was picking the oils out I was trying to recall when I was saying hello to her in the astral remembering her energy fields, which would immediately lock me into seeing if I could have her think of me in the pure way I felt in the astral. I stopped my vision, thinking it was probably not right trying to influence her subconscious through smells knowing I can do so. I let it go and just picked what really captured my attention because it was what I really wanted. I picked clove as its first oil, then birch, rosemary, and a few others that made a synergy that brought me to heaven when its therapeutic qualities centered that gorgeous beautiful aroma all around my energy field sustaining me in serenity.

A Light Worker named SKYE

Before the courtroom procedure, Lara asked to go outside and have another cigarette. I said sure as I threw on some extra essential oil hoping it's pure energetic scent would block off any cigarette smoke that drifted my way from standing next to her. We had to go by the guards again on the way back out to the exits from the security station. My eyes had gazed up in purity from a deep loving moment I had just shared with Lara and landed right directly into the soft gentle eyes that I saw in the astral of THE JUDGE as she was entering the exit we were going out of. I recognized that vibration subconsciously so fast that I had prepared a very familiar, kind hello as we passed in that eternal second. I quickly wanted to make sure she remembered the aromatherapy I used so she would remember somewhere in her being that we had met in the astral world and that I was a loving person to care for and visit my grandbaby unmonitored. It was a magical moment of recognition for me and of course confirmation. I knew I was going to see her. I called out to the angels (hers and mine) to have her look into my soul and see me. She did. It was the moment I had had purity on my face radiating from Lara's improvement! You will never tell me my higher self is not working for me 100 percent of the time behind the scenes. No one could have designed that more perfect than a supreme orchestration. I, to this day, cannot shake the memories I have of her in the astral. It melts over me as being more than once. It also melts over me that the astral I am referring to may be an actual ship.

WERE MY SUSCPISONS RIGHT?

Next I am to find out the most shocking news. They never took my grand-son's DNA test. They held him this entire time without true identification. They did not have the DNA test; there was no proof that this was even the father. They told me the only reason they had a right to take this baby from the hospital due to there being no case, was to get proper identification. They never took identification!!

** In regards to case CK9030 that you were the Judge on for the first year, I am going to make statements that I need you to hear that directly involve you. And each person on the case the first year. You are familiar with my letters and statements over the last year, conserving my vibrant passionate outpours to you and the safety of my grandson under the courts and care of DCFS LONG BEACH, supervised under the care of Erica G, Alexis A and her Lawyers. I screamed, I begged, I wrote letters. I said they are lying to you. They are lying to you I can see it.

I was wondering how often you personally participate in taking four-day-old babies from hospitals that never have been harmed WITHOUT EVEN TAKING A DNA TEST. I was wondering how one can legally take a baby and have the audacity to have a foster care agency permitted to have an unidentified infant up on websites to sell him off when he had a loving, wonderful, safe home to go to and you didn't even have a DNA TEST to begin with. ALEXIS A (the social worker I screamed at you about that you made me take orders from) NEVER TOOK A DNA TEST ON MY GRANDSON, but her lawyers told you she did anyway. The same lawyers that tried to keep me out of your courtroom, and shut the judge up when notes of my letters were highlighted, they said, "Don't bother reading it." They know they were covering up for Alexis and Erica or just didn't care? The same lawyers I screamed at you about. Alexis, before she was transferred out said to me that "Erica G" and her lawyers had said to keep me away from seeing my grandson. If you recall my frantic letters of how they illegally (insertion: or grossly) prevented me from even visiting my grandson while they were participating in selling him off without a DNA TEST AND OR A CASE, while my daughter laid in a hospital bed, while the father was unable to get to him. Facts are facts; check the records yourself, really check the date they took the DNA test. Really for the safety of our children check it yourself. They robbed and spiritually, financially, raped me and my family and my grandson from the most glorious sacred precious newborn irreplaceable moments that I never ever will get again, without even doing it legally/ Rightfully! I am a spiritual woman, and you took my Buddhist practice (of praying over our newborn) and violated my right to be a grandma over our first newborn. That was a spiritual violent robbery of a newborn and make no mistake each person will each see this in the after dimensions...I don't care what law you think you need to follow, rather than the Law of One, you are a person first before you are a judge (insertion: person? I questioned her humanness.) under our Creator. You don't have the right to violate me, period. They took a baby from the hospital with no DNA TEST AND NO HARM DONE. You made the father and our family jump through the most abusive hoops and you don't even have records. I was told point blank from Ross M, the intake ER Supervisor at DFCS, that the only right they had to take the baby was identification, and that's all (because my daughter was having a temporary lapse in memory). It didn't matter what the family had done in the past, we just needed identification. That is why we are taking the baby, which you have a safe and sacred loving home for.

That sounded reasonable. Although it's 2.5 years later, there was has been no identification established, EVER, till now, but you held him away from me anyway. You held him away anyway. The only person who caught the "lie" that I told you they were telling you was the outside worker who they said thereafter won't work for "their policy," although she was court appointed. She caught it and they shut her up. Coincidently you conveniently were taken off the case, and they transferred the social workers. Still Ms. P, there is no SSI number because it was never legal. DCFS had no right to be his parents. You violated and raped my sacred family under the honor of my grandfather who served eight years as a mayor in New York where I grew up. You disgraced my honor and my name as a respectable grandmother meeting her newborn. I remain with my statement I have always wrote you: if you or any of you in any way on case ck9030 spent one day or minute violating the right our Creator gave me to be with my grandson, there will be an entity waiting for each of you the minute you each take your last breath from this planet, taking you each down a corridor to realize your crime against humanity. Make no mistake, it will be my face seen. There is no law that will protect any of you from that. It is your personal choice to follow "the law" (decoded as the KNIGHTS OF MALTA) rather than the "Law of One." If you have any issues with that whatsoever I suggest you contact the new "COUNCIL OF TWELVE" that are now running this planet. There has been a change of guard. It comes with the Christ energy. You have just as much right as I do to approach them. Really go to prayer before you drift off to sleep, ask the holy spirit to surround you with light, and take your soul out of your body before the "Council of Twelve" state your case why you think it's okay to come in and take a baby from a home that was never harmed that had a loving safe honorable sacred spiritual home to go to! Really, they are aware of me and who I am, so tell them I sent you and tell them why you thought that was okay and why I couldn't visit our sacred newborn. Tell them all you knew about me and my life for years and my life habits so much so that you took a baby from a family. Tell them how I have acted around babies for years and how much you personally knew about me to take the baby away. Really tell them how long you knew of me and observed me and my lifestyle and my daily habits. Really tell them you took a baby from a home because the grandmother uses marijuana for medicine. Really, I want you to do that, tell them your observations of me on my real daily living routine and my stance, how I am, how I act. Tell them how you saw me every day and why it was okay to take a baby from a family. State your concerns. Really tell them, and while you are at it why don't you each tell them why you are working for the dark Kabal, putting our children in the most dangerous occult practices known to the planet, because you are. Each of you are servicing a Dark Lord. They have you so very fooled.

Let me tell you what they also did that now just terrorized every baby that ever walks through your rooms along with DCFS Long Beach and the K Foster Care agency and those specific lawyers personal hands. You know the two I talk about, the one with whopping gray curly hair, a very old crinkly face, can't miss it, and the other on the case with dark short hair, can't button his jacket full of anger with the brown Archons on them.

You each opened yourself up to the biggest darkest black underground market that there is in baby trafficking under the dark Kabal and shadow government according to what so very many of us are discovering and having evidence to now, i.e., Kenneth Annett's legal case against global baby trafficking. I have written for two years now, about where, when and how they take these babies that are taken for their annual sacrificial rituals. I told you specifically how. And they followed exactly as I wrote you about. In February of this year it was reported twice, once on Revolutionary Radio, the first week in February and from the Santos Bonacci show, the same week or thereabout. A baby was taken for their sacrificial rituals. That baby was given to the Pope, that baby was a white-skinned baby boy, that baby was born during the sacrificial months of September, October, and November as I told you, that baby was buried alive, that baby was taken from social services!...THE EXACT WAY THOSE LAWYERS ATTEMPTED TO TAKE MY GRANDSON...(check it yourself) It is the same thing. That's not going to change because we are off the case now and my grandson is home with the family recovering from the horrifying damage DCFS has done to us. Your destruction is your own network, they exist among you. I have nothing to do with the occult orders you are each under; you follow them of your own making.

A Light Worker named SKYE

**The ETs/Angels that are visiting thousands of us don't lie to us, and people are not lying to you all either. Oh my god there are so many people telling you guys the same thing. Even a "Rothschild" herself in "a Rothschild speaks out" will tell you everything I've been writing to you about, how fooled you all are. And who really you are all taking orders from. It's no secret that the United States is involved with the darker ET races. Disclosure is imminent. It is already happing in Italy's mainstream. People are risking their lives to give you all this information. If any baby is up on the K Foster Care website (including four-year-old black girls that they like making watch these rituals) and they are connected to a Catholic site, that poor baby. And to slap us all in the face they will even use Archons on someone like Erica G. or her lawyers again and/or put Erica in DCFS ER, really check where they have her. They can use her. She believes she is separate from the family's pain, like the lawyers do. The only thing a baby remembers more than anything is that you took him out of his home. Really, do the statistics. You each participate in that. The only thing a Kabal member can do is have you believe we are separate from each other, like you do in courtrooms. When each person violated me, they literally violated themselves and believing you didn't is their key to your own ethereal world. I promise you we are all ONE.*

You all terrorized me while my daughter lay in a hospital bed, made me follow the sickest rules (even registered my own car in the father's name) that separate families, tear our hearts apart, give us all PTSD with the horrors of taking our baby from our homes and your swimming and diving in occultism. And guess what, they are planning it again. They can look at what you showed them. They can do through each of you personally now, through Archon Network. There're going to start with August 15 is what we hear they start with. You let them, if you are up there taking babies in black robes at a cubical resembling "the earth" on a vortex like you all are in America. During those months, they will do it through a judge. You fall for it all. That is not a court hearing that is a designed ritual they have you do under those grid lines your court building is under, directly linking you to the dark rituals and or experiments (where you could see the bones of the babies) leading to such places as Dolce and under the Denver Airport, according to David Marshall, who you can interview for yourself who was down there. And of course the late Philip Schneider.

Letters to the Courts; Visitations...

If you are from DCFS, and you really want to protect our babies, and/or if you have a moral obligation to protect our children, research it. We alert you; don't ever, ever give a baby to a judge at a rectangular desk in a black robe during those months. That baby will be used for a ritual and they have the technology to fool each and all of you and your system. Really research what Luciferian rituals are and how they do it, what the black robe means as well as the vortex grids. These are all in place with or without me. You don't need me to tell you that everyone is putting those babies in grave danger. There is an army behind me with the same information and about changes coming to our planet. Everyone will each be informed in every angle turned. It will be in your dreamtime now, now that you have each invited yourself by yourself into a dark world.

The "supreme Light Beings," some call them Angels, many call them ETs. I expressed they are here appearing and communicating to thousands of us around the world now because of the changes that are to take place. I am not asking you to believe that. My advisers tell me not to mention that, but I already know most judges are aware of this, especially if they have ever worked up in Congress, but are under oath and cannot speak about the extensive involvement our government has with the ETs. Unfortunately not all is good. It is vibrant knowledge now in the occult world and or the real world of the truth about the darker races being above the food chain, and we humans are not at the top. You are putting babies in danger doing rituals in a courtroom where you knowingly or not are paying direct homage to the Dark Lord that pursue the "ninth circle rituals" under the grid lines.

We don't need any more Phillip Schneider getting his hand burned off and stomach gutted because he was a whistleblower who worked at the underground bases that some of these babies are taken too and handed off to their hybrid experiments of humans to Reptoids, using our children taken from the United States that places like DCFS claim the family is not fit enough to keep the baby (just like you did to me.) I was a fit honorable place for my grandson and you spend thousands of our dollars.

I explained in detail all this while Alexis complained about the length of my letters. Although there will be a day she will crave to reread every word. Instead you proved to the dark Kabal that they actually can come right in and take a white-skinned baby boy born during September,

October, November for their annual rituals and not even have a DNA test. They now know they can do it through K Foster Care's computer system, using their Archon Network. If that agency had the insane audacity to have my grandson up on a computer system even one day...(mind you, when a baby has a home, selling him off without a DNA test and violating me and my daughter while she laid in a hospital bed!) The Kabal loves that, my terror feeds them, they love that the foster care agency buys this baby trafficking because they have to take orders from a twenty-one-year-old social worker secretly working for them.

They have corrupted their entire computer system as it would be scanned now, for everyone in that black market are superior masters at fooling you all. You might want to each take note. There is an entire shadow dark group network known as the "FINDERS." They specifically hunt for white-skinned baby boys born September, October, November. They do it through the courts and DCFS. All babies in foster care are scanned by this group on the computer system first. They scan for white-skinned baby boys and hybrid potentials. The sites on which the babies are up for adaption, their technology can do this without you ever knowing, ever. This also came out from a former CIA agent named Ted (about 6 months ago). You can hear his statements on YouTube. They correlate with what I wrote you over the last year. The Archon Network uses the group of finders, they use the lawyers through the chakra system, bringing you a white-skinned baby boy to be sold off (without a DNA test). Knowingly or not those lawyers on the first year of my case are involved. They use the Archon Network that is prepared and ready. They can the Lawyers actually believe we are separate. They get in through the holes in their auras. They believe we are not one divine being under God, that is how they will continue to do it through everyone in the system. And if you sit in a room with a lawyer that has Archons on them, they will bounce on you, unless you have the spiritual armor. Wearing a black robe will violate your armor.

They upgrade the laws to detain our kids so they can be taken through judges, and the system intake is designed to take them. *I was kept away from my grandson by you because you chose to be fooled by them about those marijuana laws, but they are all making a fool of people like you. If you ever gave a baby away during those months to their rituals, they have also taken a four-year-old black girl to watch that baby you sell off or get* used for their rituals. They film it and give it to the Queen where those grid lines end. A man named David Marshall will let you know that, so look it up. Those lawyers you believe and insist on being in a courtroom, if carrying Archons on them, will bounce onto each of you if you sit next to them. Read about it yourself.

Although I cannot prove the ET stance, I have asked the ET beings and the Council of Twelve to bring to each person involved by their bedside the babies' souls that have been taken that are all under what you call "a safe system." Would you place your grandchild in that care if your child was sick?. **It's one thing to have come to me in honor to help this baby's welfare because he is in need, but it's another to violate and rape families and force us to put him in the occults.** It will not be just me I promise you. There is an army behind me with the same information. All babies born now and all Light Workers, all scientists, and many people in Washington that are Light Beings are going to be making sure you are aware.

I signed like I signed all my letters: A Light Worker named Skye!

Letter to the Lawyers****You know who I am, I am going to get right to the point. Your life is about to change. You defended Children's Services for coming in and taking a four-day-old baby from the hospital without a case and now we know, without even identification. You participated in taking a baby that was never harmed, that had had a loving sacred home arranged while his mother laid in a hospital bed with an illness. You worked with Supervisor Erica G. and Alexis A. You even participated in keeping my visits intentionally at bay. Let me tell you the results of your grand work.*

I know you have read my letters, therefore you understand the seriousness of the dark Kabal, the shadow government running our Planet with the Vatican being one infrastructure working with the Reptoids that are in human form. I have explained to you I am a Light Worker genetically coded to have my memory returned to me. That is part of the Akashic memory. We have abilities to leave our bodies if the Angels, the ET, or the Guardians of our planet wish us to be informed about something. There are thousands of us now around the planet and growing day by day. It was a request from our supreme Creator because we are at the end of linear time; equally most babies now will be born with these understandings. They are preparing us for vast changes. I have gone into detail, long detail. I took my time and energy writing endless letters. You may want to review them. They will directly affect you and your family. I have explained to you at the risk of sounding insane how, where, and when these Alien Reptoids came onto our planet and how they have intermingled with humanity even disguising themselves in human forms. I have explained to you that the Reptoids believe they own this planet. I have explained to you that many of our leaders, authority figures, judges, and elites are not even people, and/or are mingling with other races in one fashion or another. Some are what was prophesized to us in a very many scriptures including the Bible, the Nag Hammadi, and the rest of our scriptures that were intentionally burned in the libraries of ancient Alexandria. They work through the Archon Network. The Archon network will also use our leaders and judges to control this planet if needed.

I have explained to you that if you yourself trace every building in Washington, D.C, that is a major US building, you will trace a pentagram and that pentagram is facing down. I have explained that underneath most major churches—churches with daycare facilities, court houses—are all strategically placed on grid lines where underneath they are fed the food of human terror and/or their actual live flesh as we again are not the top of the food chain. Usually, this is done through their sacrificial ritual of babies, many babies, especially white-skinned baby boys, predominately of Jewish blood, during their sacrificial honor months of September (9/11), October, November. I have explained to you all that our government keeps this from us because many of them have used some of the darker Alien races to get technology and means for warfare, including space warfare, in exchange for experimenting on humans, mainly children. Especially now as our current government has made a deal to exchange humans/children for the current technology from a star that sends out waves, allowing Earth to go interdimensional with blank slate technology. It is imperative that this technology does not get in the wrong hands. You personally contribute to that worshiping what you do. Every judge does who wears a black robe. That is an occult fact that is not my opinion. I have explained to you these children are taken through social services and all other organizations where the state is funding. I explained what Alien groups are working with our government, the good and the bad as there are groups of both. I have explained to you where they are and where they do their sacrifices. I wrote forever. I alarmed you all but again last year there was a baby taken in the United States from Social Services, the people you defend. That baby was a white-skinned baby boy taken during their sacrificial months. It was reported twice, and you can hear the verbiage yourself on Revelation Radio (insertion: check the archives as shortly after my letter the station was taken down, although the archives run) as well as the other references I gave you the first week of February. That baby was given to the Pope and buried alive. I have explained to you where in the United States these children are taken to and experimented on for the hybrid Reptoid humans that they are trying to turn humanity into. Today, as we are, hundreds are taken not just one here and there. They are held hands tied to bars. (reference: Basis 37 Sahara Adams). They are electrified to death during these experiments so that they can see how much each race can handle. All babies and children missing are taken there. There is not one person missing that the Alien races haven't taken for these experiments, unless one of our good Alien races interferes for help, such as sections of the Raptors that save most humans from the human the raids as some of the Reptoids, do.

All babies now in the United States, once in the system, the system that you defend, once up on the computer system, such as my grandson, who was at K Foster Care, are scanned, scoped out, and, if they like that baby, they will get him and most likely a black little girl to watch either their sexual acts or their actual rituals. They are given to many Freemasons and many leaders. If they are not given to Congressmen, they are handed over to the underground bases in the United States. They do it through the Archon Network that works with the Reptoids that works with a race called the Trogs. (refer to: Kerry Cassidy Project Camelot, with Mark Richards) Both want humans off this planet, all part of a Nazi network that is alive and well. The Archon Network you feed, they are swimming in your auric field. I can see it on you both and the social workers; you're all wrapped in the trance.

Unfortunately many leaders (judges) are framed. They think they are going to a party, then their pictures are taken while being at the ritual. If they speak they or their families are murdered. Many judges are under their trap, and or either mind controlled through MK Ultra. They have the technology to fool you, everyone of you. The Illuminati members, who in secret call themselves a different name, worship the black Sun. All judges are paying homage to them when they wear their black robes deliberately depicting direct symbolism decoded from the black sun worshipers. All citizens are sworn in under the Dark Lord of this planet. They made sure you carried the mark of the beast and we all have to obey or we are set in jail with the cops equally under their spell. Equally so, in Luciferian symbolism, of the Dark Lord running our planet, is the practice of wearing a black robe that is hovering over a raised desk in a square or rectangular shape. Both represent the homage and the ritual. That is a symbol of Earth. I could explain how but there will be an army behind me explaining this to you. I have also already given references to everything. Sometimes angels take us to their meeting, the meeting of the dark elites. They don't have good plans for humans. I do not trust these Reptoids with Jews. It's the same race that is here, the same Alien race that Hitler worked with. Only they are way more cleaver, sneakier, and their holographic technology is impeccable. Obviously, you all have been so fooled. They operate in the ethereal. You cannot see it because you are in a courtroom tearing families apart, right where they want you. They also want gay judges in family courtrooms, a gay judge telling families how to be when they don't even procreate. We will see a large number of gay judges and leaders now; this is intentional. They do not want any more population; they do not have enough SSI income. Most chemical trails out now are pouring out hormones for gay tendencies. They do not want families together. They want humans depopulated. Trust me and watch a rise in gay leaders. The presidents are picked years before. Everything out there is a lie and everyone goes gung ho on these elections. Lawyers, politicians, are so fooled. The military, although are spot on, there are some leaders in there that are participating in our freedom; they are working with the benevolent ETs. No one will ever be able to detect that.

I explained to you that those are not courtroom procedures you participate in when you go to a courtroom that is under a vortex (all courthouse are on some sort of vortex). They are designed rituals and there is a whole dark demonic race sucking up the dark energy someone feels when they lose a case, any case although especially when a child is taken and someone loses. They love the terror of families. They love that when a baby is *set out for adoption that they know they will end up with that child one way or another if they want him or her. Most are through the Catholic or Christian adaption centers. The ones you defend when you want to take a baby from a home. They are an infrastructure with the dark entities running the Vatican. The same energy under the White House is the same demonic energy I felt under the Vatican. The Christians are so fooled and they are good people. The Catholic mass is the epitome of the worship of the Dark Lord. Even the day they have as Jesus's birthday is the highest occult day of the Dark Lord. They love that many people see what I see and you all are fooled. They are masters at putting themselves in disguise. That's how they get our children. It's easy to fool the social workers; they are so brainwashed almost as much as they are at K Foster Care and most foster care agencies that are using Catholic adoption centers. I explained to you there was a group of people that work a organization for the dark Kabal called the Finders that the CIA again, as well as others such as Cathy O'Brien and her doctor, discovered, describing them working secretly underground scanning all supposed stray babies through the social service systems and alike. This is namely babies for pedophilia acts as well as sacrificial rituals done by our leaders and the Reptoids. Although now the children will be traded for the new technology I described.* Insertion: Simon Park who is known to be part of the Reptiods himself (I believe 1/4 is what he states)/whistleblower/politician, will also confirm that the organizations such as DCFS and the orphanages are in place for the sole purpose to use our children for their alien need, any need. It's quiet deep to listen to his interviews. He also shape shifts in some mild manner I believe, although this is not uncommon. It's imperative to listen to this information.

It's all one satanic infrastructure and you goddamn people forced me to hand over my grandson to the sickest baby trafficking scheme on the planet. And guess what, they're going to do it all over again this year starting Aug 15 (see again Kenneth Annette's legal case against global baby trafficking done through the courts,) then into the sacrificial months. They will do it through a judge; you provoke them and they pay you good for it, which is intentional. You participate in the destruction of humanity every time you honor a person in a black robe taking babies. You said stuff about me in the courtroom and you never met me, you bastards. You were taking a newborn out of a loving home and you haven't even met me. How in God's name can you live with yourself? You all knew goddamn well I had a wonderful home for my grandson, although you will honor that system before you honor your brother and sister. That is how the Archon Network lives in your bodies and attaches to your aura. And the Archon Network will continue to use you. They will also bounce onto a social worker or a judge if you are in a room with them. They love that you guys bring terror to a family. This is going to continue at a high rate now as these beings are being released rapidly. They cling to you all in courtrooms, they love you, then they will spit you out, and I hope I will be the first to spit on you and I hope to God my grandson joins me.

The Law that you defend is decoded as the Knights of Malta. That's the Jesuits. They work with the Dark Lord. You are all under their spell. You can call all this crazy but one thing you will never be able to do is prove me wrong. You are directly linked to a baby trafficking scheme. I would not want to be you or your family once disclosure happens on the planet, and there will be disclosure. You also violated me and my grandson. You raped our time together, and I promise you when our Creator has put a family together you don't have the right to barge in like you think you do, tell my family how to conduct life when you honor the dark Kabal the way you do, and your own life habits are horrific. You have been horribly fooled. Although in your left brain mind I can't prove anything, but what I can do and have done and will participate in is making sure all the souls that social services and government organizations, that have been used one way or another, either dead or alive, be brought to everyone of your bedsides in the middle of the night. I hope you are all watched by your peers because you all may be coming to work very tired.

If this were an isolated case that happened even once under our government, I believe every single person needs to seize all operations without exception, game over, step aside. Every one of you there, everyone, all day care facilities and foster cares and agencies under the United States, all of them, every last one of them, all judges in black robes, that is therefore what we would do in a normal crime scene, although it has happened so very many times and it vibrantly continues. I could not put on a black robe and call myself an honorable person, Many judges who are aware of this *(which is growing more and more) won't anymore and anyone who does is either under the trance or directly working for the Kabal and or a Reptoid themselves. We see their skin peel often ya know. Unfortunately for the Reptoids they are not all bad. I would be appalled at myself being a lawyer sitting there like a monkey tearing families apart, taking orders from an organization that's about to kill mankind one way or another, starting with Jews. The only way a child will be safe is if all children are 100 percent out of a courtroom under the United States of America; there is no other statement than that. There are now many leaders who are aware of what I tell you; they absolutely refuse to participate. The rest of you carry the mark of the beast.*

I will tell you like I told everyone else on the case, I will never harm nor come near you. I don't need to do a thing to watch your karma. I can see it from here without leaving home but what I will say is the second after you take your last breath, when you leave this planet, there is an arranged entity to come meet your soul to take you down a corridor, you're going to be shocked. You will then see my face you bastards. Get up and go to work tomorrow; there is a baby again about to be used or murdered.

I am a Light Worker for this planet named Skye

After I wrote the letter(s) I felt such relief. I needed them to know the truth or confront them if they already knew it. I felt like I could breath. Even after all I screamed and wrote, though, I still felt I had held in so much. With my esoteric knowledge I would lie in bed at night pretty much convinced that these people had targeted my grandson for their rituals or experiments, especially now. There is real time trading going on with our the ET races and our children, we have all the proof we need, not only with the whistleblowers coming forth but people like me where I was awaken at night getting information from the Light Beings that lead me to all this to begin with. I had a damn good reason to go vibrant with my letters, this wasn't some random fear. It is also increasingly common I am learning to take a baby that has a mother who has been Mind Controlled. (I will forever keep Cathy O'Brien's daughter in my chants).

Does all this sound extreme? Oh no, let me repeat, oh hell no. You make no mistake reader of what the darker side has been involved in right here on this planet and not some far off theory. There is immense proof. Ten miles down the road from where my grandson was at the Foster Care, was were one of these happenings took place. (Reference Cathy O'Brien and her Doctor, there is a YouTube interview of the facility). Does it happen all the time? No, although if it happens at all in any form it needs to be emphasized, that is how I see it. Knowledge is power and also very healing.

The light as I always said makes me aware of the dark even though I wish I could have stayed oblivious and innocent to all this and for a good reason, I thought. Most people don't want to know the truth. I think that is bullshit. I don't think we as humans that truly recognize our oneness have the right to turn the other cheek. If enough of us unite this will cease, although it is a trick of the dark to get lost and not be seen, for all things will be healed in the light. I would rather the world condemn me as crazy than stand by and watch another ritual or another promotion to the darker energies in anyway shape or form, period.

CHAPTER 22
THE SUPREME CREATOR IS !

The baby's father called me from jail. He has been tamed quite a bit by the influence of others in there that are connected to Jesus. He explained how his savior has touched his being and wants nothing more than to be sober and with his son and family. According to his prior letter and according to the conversation he is 100 percent on board for keeping and bringing his baby home, excited to be clean, and is complying with all conditions sent to him from the courts.

He was right. The father stood by his spiritual awakening and his sacred path. He got clean and sober and turned his life around. He went step by step and followed everything he was supposed to do. They broke so many rules against him as well. They went out of their way to take the baby from him. He was stunningly powerful and very humbled. He took it all with grace. He brought the baby home after 2.5 years.

My grandsons utter preciousness, joy and angelic spirit is just spread all over me these days! It has taken a while for me to be off guard to wonder if someone is going to come in and rip him from our lives again. I believe I was so traumatized it will linger in me the rest of his life, having the state come in and kidnap him from me. That was kidnap, that will be on their soul when they leave the planet. They took a baby against a families will. He had a safe spiritual home. They will have to walk through this pain themselves before they are united with the Oneness! No one ever gets away with anything ever, not in spirit world, you do not break the Law of One!

A Light Worker named SKYE

Below is the **end** of the letter that had been sent to *several of the judges* at once at the Edmunds Children Court here in Los Angeles. The beginning of the letter was placed in the Archon Chapter, some of the middle is above and here is the end. It's important to put things back in true perspective. In true reality there is the Supreme and the truth of the grand process in play. I took an awful long time explaining the dark for the purpose of knowledge and more knowledge to arm you with what you need but make no mistake the Supreme will reign. Planet Earth and her children are headed for something very magnificent. This is what we must prepare ourselves for.

*** I am going to explain the Resistance Movement." It is a fulfillment of the galactic prophecy. The restoration plan consists of highly intelligent beings many members and organizations on and off planet Earth, ET, human, and ascended spiritual masters. It's a far superior plan with superior technology far greater than you could almost imagine. Consisting of the following but now limited to: Members of Agartha—beings from the center of the earth, spiritually high-based societies (many from Lemuria and Atlantis after the fall—the flood of those civilizations). Also the Council of Immortals and ascended masters and our twenty-four Elders; Shambala/Shambawa have confirmed this with me. (Shambala, Shambawa I later learned were real, with the underground Agarthiens) They were the second that reassured me of this restoration plan. In addition to Agartha there is the entire Galactic Federation, that consists of 140 star systems and three hundred planets based out of Telsede. From there is the Adrominin Council of Light and the Orion Council of Light, and many Light Workers are from both. The Plaedians, (insertion: not all Plaedians), the Acturians (who's ships of light I personally believe are here at the four corners of the earth). There are also ascended masters from the Melchizedic Order, which is the Order of the (original) Christ energy. Moses is also from the Melchizedic Order and many other masters. Also this includes Planet X. (insertion: planet x means different thing to different people) We are all connected to the same telepathic radar. There are also surface based beings, what is called the White Nights, consisting of members in our CIA our police force and our military. There is also an agreement that hundreds of thousands of police officers have signed to protect us people rather than the government. I assure you there is a designed plan to restore our planet far* greater than you know and it will happen; we are given missions accordingly. We are all awaiting the time. Many of us have incarnated for this. Once this takes place and all banking systems and Internet structures are shut down, a restoration plan will be carried out. The judges that did not participate with the Kabal will be going into healing chambers with the citizens is what many understand. You will understand that you do not disarm dysfunctional behaviors until you experience them yourself. You literally have to walk through the pain you have caused each person. There is no escaping the law of one that we will all be operating on. You will not be let out into society until your debt to humanity is paid. Your vibration will not move your cells. The Sun is sending its solar raise to us from creation itself, igniting our DNA. Harm is a low vibration, and it carries a color and a frequency if you will. It goes in density. Everyone will see these colors and frequencies on you in the next dimension. They carry vibration particles that resonate of taking a baby from a family unwillingly (harmfully and hurtfully in my case). It is considered a crime listed in the "hall of records," a crime against humanity, which is what you people do. We are all one. It will resonate a low frequency causing dark beings around your soul that carry the screams of a like vibration, (We are energy beings). That's what will resonate and attach to you. It is that serious and we are that divinely connected. You will be made to understand and operate under the LAW OF ONE; you will not escape this. All of our galactic family in all the solar system operates under this Universal Law. Anyone who has been taken out of the Matrix will tell you this, and if have been taken out of the Matrix that is the only time you would utter the words YOUR HONOR. I promise you there would be no baby snatching from families. You will learn other methods of correction. You wouldn't even think twice to work at a place like Children Services. You will understand that will violently directly affect "you." There is no escaping that. You are going to find this out firsthand, each of you.

Before the planetary restoration and economic plans allowing us to not only have access to our once guarded star gates (of course underground Iraq) Himalayans, etc., take place, at which time we will be introduced to free energy. All monies will be returned to the public that was robbed from them from the elites. (Most likely we will not use the current monetary system.) And the gold igniting our DNA has been moved and protected at the center of the earth now. We will also be introduced to ways that will expand our lives and rejuvenate our chi, our energy field through solar chi where we live for far greater length of lives, as the prime Creator did not make junk. I have my partial memory back of this society. We will return to this; I have been assured of this. We will never even think of killing an animal to eat, we will not consider murder of this kind in these civilizations. There is an actual animal kingdom.

In the meantime it is imperative we protect the children, as things are going to change. You must understand what you are dealing with. Nothing hurts and terrorizes the planet more than people in law dealing with the occults. Because you refuse to admit they are separate, (the law and the kabal are ONE) they use you, through your ego and your need to separate one from the next rending duality, separateness—one wins ones loses. **The occults use the law because lawyers are the least educated on the occults** and they manipulate your ego every way possible to keep you in disguise and fighting each other. They even provide a great income for you. Law also does not know spirit world and the black magic has therefore taken over because all law underneath is run by the Jesuits. They work with the dark Alien races, again the same ones who worked with Hitler. It's a long kind of war between Annunaki brothers (that would be another letter involving Hebrews and the Torah).

Once our Galactic Family interacts with us there will be many restoration plans. Children will be placed with the indigenous cultures that work with officials that are of a high order. The way we do it now would be a disgrace and dismantled in a nanosecond; everyone in the higher evolved societies are very well aware you do not succeed on one end and terrorize on the other, thinking you are not going to be directly affected yourself down the line. We also can see auras and frequencies that tell us everything about you. Live scanning and the old fashioned paperwork you people do would be something the teenagers will read about in a comic nightmare about Planet Earth.

Checking energy fields/auras with the new camera's out now (I think Europe and here in Los Angeles) created to see the auras hence identifying these Leeches and identifying Archons. This will tell you much of everything you need to know in keeping a baby safe during these times. Each center

THE SUPREME CREATOR IS !

reveals a different pattern and if that person has a Leech on them that is directed to the darker realms, it will show. It will also give each person a direct opportunity for healing. You must have your energy field clean before you even consider having any say whatsoever in any manner whatsoever regarding children and decision making. That means the judges, all workers, all lawyers, all foster care agencies, and anyone transporting children. I will tell you that if you are in courtrooms and foster cares taking babies from homes the way you people do, you will not have a clear field. It doesn't work that way. It will take massive work to clear. You have to go back and make amends to every person you have harmed. Spiritually, emotionally physically, financially. That's just one Chakra. It goes in many layers. Every dot on an I and every T will be accounted for. In order to rid one of a Leech and the Archons one needs the help of Light Workers and ascended masters or a profound spiritual experience of one's understanding.

One more thing you must know about the Archons and the Leeches and their descents on planet and off planet is they hate Light Workers. They know we can sense them. They literally have a different blood energy smell. It is massively deceitful that you often feel very secure around them with their false power and structures. They know who we are, and they go out of their way to destroy us on planet and off planet. They do not want you to have the information we give you. They work through Archons and Leeches as hidden controllers to destroy us and our families, our business, our computers. They also do not like that many are trained to depower them. A man named Robert Stanley is well educated with the government's involvement using these Leeches and Archons and how they attach them to workers and government workers. They vibrantly do it through you judges. They literally use you to destroy light formation. In working for these Archons they even come to you in your dreams. They are in the astral, (the fourth dimension, the fourth is the collective) they hover over each of you. If you are involved with courts around children, they are there. You must get real about this, unless each vortex pattern/Chakra is clear in your body. The darker forces also understand that the angelic /galactic family, etc., have not lost their powers like they have when they fell from Heaven. The dark forces are rulers of this planet right now, they have threaten to continue to omit mankind if the benevolent beings interfere. They use you. Some of them are you.

A Light Worker named SKYE

My grandfather was the Mayor of the city in New York where I grew up for eight years. My brother worked for the Senate. I have community in my blood. But more so I have been touched by creation itself. I will not go back to my Creator not doing my job for this planet. I will not stop my work and preparing the way for our ascended master to return. I have had enough attention from the UFO (UFology) and spiritual communities of which are having me help share the information on these topics where I am doing radio shows also exposing what I went through at Long Beach Children Services, and what the courts are involved in. We must educate and unite each other about what is really going on with our children here. As well we must prepare for the return of the light now; our signs have been given around the planet. (Insertion: The Kabal are also following a bible script before the return of the true Light.)

CHAPTER 23

OTHER CONTACTEE'S
ALONG THE WAY!

My soul felt and continues to feel a huge relief sticking up for myself, and of course I did it with no back up, which made my inner being excel more. Me against an empire. No one knew the hell I went through with the system except if you have been there yourself to this extent. Oh, and so very many have! My prayers and chants are with them every morning. There is not a Light Worker on this planet that hasn't had a prayer sent their way through me.

Often, on the other end of feeling powerful as my letters to the courts and the owners of children's services continued, with all the information I had, I felt utterly insane. How could I be this single girl alone out here with all this information and possibly fit in anywhere. Really, anywhere in the normal social circles. Really, except for my sweet dad, even my family thinks I am out there. Anyone would who is not exposed to this stuff. On the other had if you have been exposed to this stuff you will find immense accuracy and/or profound similarities. I felt crazy. Really my best friends did not understand me but did keep me grounded.

Dating for me was insane. It pretty much went like this before I always came home alone. "Hi, I'm Skye." I would continue on my normal way. "I am a Light Worker from another planet and I talk to ETs and Angels. Quick let me tell you about the dark Aliens running the show and how they have my daughter's soul and perhaps even have an eye on her to have her son to be taken for the baby sacrificial rituals they do here in the US. I don't watch TV. I don't eat meat. I don't engage in society's ways." It was a nightmare because I was utterly bored with their world of TV and minor insane conversations of the gossiping of people and waking up every day to go full speed ahead fitting themselves into an insane society. They, I believe, thought I was pretty but crazy as I caught on. I think they even felt sorry for me, for my deranged mind wanting to blame Aliens, the Government, DCFS, or whatever for my difficult life with my daughter. I kept myself very grounded going on hikes. I think I have walked around the city even more than a meth addict walks around in their daze.

I had to play devil's advocate to myself often. I asked myself often, Was I blaming Children Services for everything while all they were trying to do was protect my grandson? Was I trying to state a huge case just to prove I am right and their judgments were wrong? The only thing I knew was my gut was on fire when they took my grandson.

To this day I stand by my convictions and treble for the children that are taken by the DCFS, especially in the US, Brussels and London. The people must be educated and unite. Light Workers and Ascended Masters are doing this as fast as we can. We need your help. Please if any of this rings true to you, send my writings out to someone that may benefit. It is torturous to have a parent sit there in their pain not knowing there is more. There is so much help coming forth. There are conferences and panels and people and support groups to help. Keep in touch with me, I will keep you posted. You will never be alone on your journey. We are one you and I. I send you all the strength you need when you forget that you have your own. I believe I was shown all of this for a divine reason. A part of the whole recovery. Many people are doing their parts, those letters of awareness to the courts were my part of my piece in repairing the Whole, the One.

What I did know is playing hierarchy to judges and a failing system is not my design of thinking. The system breeds duality and separation. I have no value in a judge unless that judge is a spiritual leader caring for the wisdom of all the worlds and universes and that their connection to spirit would be so impeccable that they could see your soul and your soul mission. Then, I will value their opinion. I hold that stance, as I believe everyone should. Our indigenous cultures go to our spiritual wise elders and ascended masters for such matters, while we have all agreed and succumbed to a "system," a satanic one at that, to solve these matters that has done way more harm than good when it comes to people correction. "People" are the last priority in the "system." Having the Courts involved in family matters is a hardship for humanity and I believe we greatly need to revise this. I also understand with what I have been shown by the "light" is that all manners such as this will be attended to during the "Golden Age." Remember these words and you may remember me. Children **will** be taken out of that satanic system and be brought to loving, safe, nurturing environments without sacrificial threats and without families being terrorized. That system will no longer exist as we enter the New Golden Age and continue to awaken to our Oneness! It will not sustain the vibration of Creator God.

The planet was and is changing. I have been "AWAKENED" to see this change in a very profound way. I was interacting and or traveling more and more with LIGHT WORKERS and scientists as well as spiritual leaders all around the world that are coming up with the same answers. I know that science and spirituality must be met and incorporated into these governmental organizations or they will collapse on themselves not being able to keep up with the higher vibrations that are without a doubt entering our planet. I knew that the two worlds must be met if we were to continue with an operating civilization.

One of my favorite places I went to was the James Gilliland Ranch in Washington State. He is known all over the world for his ECETI Ranch. We hung out for hours and watched the ET ships. We would send them loving energy and they would beam their lights and power up for us. The land is a vortex point, a portal between dimensions. Besides the sighting of thousands of ships there also have been sightings of very high masters known to be that of Mother Mary, as shown by the pictures of her sitting inside the meditation building next to other pictures of our star beings from different places.

A very magical fairytale thing for me that I was in utter tears about was when I saw the orbs. The orbs were everything to me. I knew they were real because they told me they were real in all our communications through their contact with me. My communication with the ETs and Master was a bit different than some contactees but very real. I had communication of a clairaudio, or advance telepathy better explained, telepathy from other dimensions. This is the basic way we do it in other dimensions. To confirm that my communication is indeed in process, they literally flutter at my nose and face. James, being impeccably intuitive and of course having his own dialogue with these beings much, much, longer than I had, immediately said (during one of our clearing sessions) my nose, I feel my nose twitch. I began to even more understand my connection to it all. It was also a charm for me because I didn't feel so god-damn crazy. The normal language at the ranch was about ET, Grays, Yates, Tall Whites, Archons, Ascended Masters. I walked around the meadow out in front where all the sightings were feeling understood, not only about all these things but also understood when I mentioned the Archons. Amazingly enough James was real familiar with them and had actually been writing about them since the 80s. I melted with relief as we shared similar information. I was also given a fabulous clearing.

What also made me fall to utter amazement is later when I went home I kept recalling the way these orbs fluttered from one end of the sky to the other in odd shapes. Why are you guys doing this I kept thinking to myself? Why are they flying in these odd shapes that are making them go outside of the "sky" binoculars that James had. I was kind of mad at them for doing that. I wanted to follow them smoothly. They went back and forth one end of the sky looping around with another at the other end of the sky. You guys what are you doing? I telepathically sent them messages. I did not get a response. Oh well, this is insanely incredible anyway, I thought. I continued on for two nights and every ship was like the first. The next day there was a cloud disk that I had filmed and put on my Enlighten Beings YouTube channel that was above the mountain, Mount Adams. The ET ships were there behind the Cloud Disc, clearing out the chemical trails. I recall how these ships sat there and hovered over the mountain very much like I saw when I went to Mount Shasta. That of course is a main vortex point on Planet Earth. I went there during the Venus Transit. I believe this was kind of the conception point where Gaia Mother Earth was met by the return of some masters including Quizimoto as explained by the Mayans. Conception point, where the masters passed the firmament, the gate over planet earth. That was how I understood it anyway.

In my inner world I am wanting to understand these beings and where they're from. Our system or the fallen, I wondered, as I always wonder in thought. But I felt the light coming to Earth. I felt this was the break into it all at least from a planetary perspective. From there the birthing pains on our planet would start. I do not know earth's incubation period before the birth of the light or the return of the Ascended Masters, none of us do, but we understand we must prepare for the light. This of course was just one sign. It was very much like when the three Wiseman followed the stars (or are the stars) to the birth of a new age or a Christ. There were also signs increasing in the Middle East and around the Earth that had been prophesied: the Pope resigning and the "Prophecy of Malachi," NWO signs, Femma camps being built. Currency changes. The signs were here, and it was time to prepare for the light I saw, and it lingered(s) in my being day and night. I missed my Creator, I missed being home with God as I knew Mother-Father God or Prime Creator, the Light, the Love.

Shortly after I returned home from the ranch during one of my morning sessions with the Light Beings I kept reviewing in my head the odd shape the orbs were doing in the sky. They kind of gave me a chuckle. I didn't get it. I just wished they stayed inside the view of the binoculars. Oh my God! I screamed at myself, Oh my God! I screamed at myself again and then bounced off my bed recalling that before I left I asked these beings if they would do something fun for me that I would notice. I laughed at them kind of mooching them saying all right guys maybe you could do something real cool like throw purple hearts in the sky, thinking that will never even almost happen. I'm just playing magic kind of "prove yourself" ego games with them. From one end of the sky an orb made a loop symbolizing half of a heart, from way on other end came another orb tracing the sky shaping it filling in the other half of the heart. They did this several times for me. They sent me my heart!

There have been many places and people I have met and adored. Another, Carol Rosslyn who was at Contact In the Desert in Joshua Tree, the first year, she so passionate and bravely speaks of the Secret Space Program and how we are fooled to weaponize space according to Colonel Von Braun, who she'd work for in the Secret Space Mission way back; shouting to us all "There is an agenda! The last card, the fake Alien invasion from space!

I did a little video clip with and for her talking about our Galactic Family and how their actions will be nil. Those ET races are so evolved, and space weapons to them are a joke. We are all One even with the ETs. That clip, I was told, went to fourteen of our world leaders. If I know Carol, it got there. I also let those leaders of our world know that whatever choices they made they were indeed going to come back and relive it all first hands themselves.

A Light Worker named SKYE

Later that week after going to bed and reviewing on YouTube more information about Colonel Von Braun, I asked the Light Beings if what he spoke of was real. In the middle of the night his YouTube video powered up on my sleeping computer out of now where, his voice is waking me from my dream state! I got my answer alright.

CHAPTER 24

REALITY TODAY

When I think of Lara now I understand that she could snapped out of this at any minute. Sometimes she does. Yes that is very real. Today this day during my writing journey with you over the last three years, this particular day I will tell you this, today my daughter called me direct and coherent, fully identified me as her mother. It came out of the blue. I have done everything I learned with dealing with these Archons and have put it into practice this whole time. I absolutely know that there is a supreme light Christ energy that does and will heal. I am seeing it. It has taken immense help but today my daughter was back 100 percent. She said that "THE LAW" has released her. I kept asking if it was real. She said it was real and she wanted to see me. I said back to her that I was actually concerned that if I went to see her by the time I got there THE LAW would get mad at her because they said I am not your mother. My daughter then said to me "Well we know that's not true." At that instant a huge smile came on my face and a flutter of warmth in my heart more so because she then asked me for a hairpiece. She then after that asked me if she could have it now. Well that would be my daughter; that is correct. She wants everything right now. I laughed because I knew that that was the only way she would have came back, with the vibrant Lara personality.

Lara sounds great today. Lara is here today with us. I am not going to question this. I don't want to analyze or figure out or go on a search for another damn thing. I just want to look at her. I just want to look at my daughter. She is here now as we step forward and set out into the next set of journeys in our lives, learning, wondering how long she will remain. Her mind was brilliant before. I see those cells repairing here. We will take this one day, one step at a time as the recovery is not an overnight process, knowing that she truly needs to be nurtured in her fullest to have her Chakra centers protected from now on. Then we can deal with the back-to-normal behaviors of interacting; what a quality problem that is to me. **Come now, mom!**

She actually improved so much she left the facility or was downgraded to a more or open transitional life. I believe the downgrade was way too soon for her to combat the addiction she has. I never got to see her out of the lockdown facility. I became used to the roller coaster ride and just loved her anyway. The last time we saw her we held her in a nice Christmas visit with her son. That was almost a year ago now. I have not seen my daughter in a year. I can't write here anymore words to describe what that feels like. I've already said them. She does not claim her family to be real, and they will not let me have contact with her whatsoever due to her sudden and urgent request. I was never granted conservatorship of my own daughter therefore not privy to confidential information. They can't give me conservatorship if she doesn't know me is what they tell me. Taylor does not acknowledge the family. Lara on the other hand loved her family, and she and I were very close. My mind goes back to her telling me all she ever wanted was a baby.

In court, I heard by chance the doctor stating that since her downgrade she was not doing good. The judge from the mental courts facility wanted me to speak with her doctor when they were investigating my request for conservatorship. He again told me the words I dread to hear, "Your daughter is very sick!" In truth, it's just different now when I hear those words. I am armed with knowledge. I am armed with the light of Supreme Creator. I can see far beyond this third-dimensional world. There is no need for me to fear. I have been trained to understand this. I also have been trained to understand there was going to be healing of all our diseases not just the removal of the Archons and dark Kabal on the planet once the Higher Supreme energy arrives. It is arriving. We are preparing for this. Her father was very, very sick and later in life rebuilt himself as best as he could. His once very sick mind came back. Their condition was so similar in so many ways, right down to even being in the same mental hospital, as I stated, while they were both born in different states. I have seen so many hopeless addicts that have been taken over by Archons and not even recognize it as such and recover fully with the Supreme energy. Once the energy field is clear in her Chakra system and the Christ energy of the Supreme takes over her, there will be no room for sickness. The Archons, the Electronic Harassment and the Addiction itself cannot live in a spirited house. Do I believe she will come back again. Oh yes, I do. I've seen it, I've seen her come back 100 percent. That's a tall order from where she came. I have so much faith in her. Really, there was no way I ever thought she would ever even carry on a conversation, let alone be released. I am so proud of her. She inherited bad genes from her father and my mother. I saw her over coming it all, it was insane and so power-ful. As if she was chosen to be the powerful one to wash all the mental illness away from our family cycle. Really, to overcome electronic harassment and the Archons that had entered her the way she did is a God Damn miracle. There is recovery from electronic harassment, even with someone who has a handler like I have been shown my daughter has had. Solaris Blue Raven also was able to overcome the Mind Control/Electronic Harassment because spirit within her made a statement. (Her handler is known to be from the band "Rush!") My daughter did this, she overcame this because she's amazing. I send her the DNA signals from mine, so does the Christ energy. She catches that. My next set of prayers is that once she clears again, she will stay clear. I believe this is a process as well. One I am not in control of!

I also believe in my daughter because I've seen her father snap out of his supposed paranoid schizophrenic periods to never have them again ever. Telling me years later it was all Crystal Meth. "It was all Crystal Meth" he repeats, not schizophrenia **Meth is the Devils Drug used by the elites to open ones portal to electronically control a person**. These are facts. Drug users must be aware of this. It is not just taking drugs anymore people. Unless my daughter decides to play out her mission on another planet, which of course is always an option for a soul, I believe in her return. I believe in her return because I have seen horrific addicts recover. There are "Archons in the Addicts" (which was my alternate title version) and they are still recovering. I believe she will return because I have seen it firsthand myself. No sign of men-tal illness or electronic harassment and fully present and that was after all that horrific damage. I believe in her full recovery even from the supposed mental illness, because in my heart of heart of hearts I do not believe she suffers from mental illness, fully, I believe she suffers more of from a spiritual malady. Not of a permanent kind. I believe she will recover because I believe in the

Supreme. I know we are not limited. I know this. I believe she will return when and only when she herself is ready

It is a decision made between Lara and Supreme Creator when her spirited house arrives; but it will arrive, it's not my decision when on her soul journey she decides to chose her light. I love her anyway. Her inner self knows exactly what it is doing. I can see it in her eyes. I also understand that there was no way a soul would ever go that low without ever going back that immensely high. She is and will be held in the arms of Creation throughout eternity. I have been shown this in a visualization that came to me not once but several times…

I am going to tell you something beautiful about my precious daughter. In fact, it is the reason I talk about "A" path to enlightenment, rather than "my." I mention the concept of the soul expanding through the dark. This is what we are all up to, a path of enlightenment, that is why we are all here. I was able in my mind, during my very special walk I had today with the Light Beings, communicating with me sending me this message. I was able to tap into a timeline or dimension that was able to visit my daughter's soul. I saw her there. I recognized her essence like it was mine. She was an Angel, a literal angel of light in a human body. You knew it when you walked by her. The community she was in, she was actually a profound spiritual leader and looked upon with purity because of her essence. I saw her essence there. I recognized her as I do when I travel. Her soul was so pretty. It was frustrating not being able to run and hug her being my daughter, stopped boldly by the sudden clear waves of the timeline; I was standing in the crowd watching her up there healing and speaking to the sick. Thousands would gather and see her. I knew she would shine. I knew that she would be the Enlightened One. I knew the light of the world and I knew my Creator was going to carry her home. They showed me this today! A holy day today!

That is what I remember. I re-member with the whole as Neal Donald Walsh says in his conversations with Gods Book or Creators Book through him. We re-member our oneness. I remember Lemuria. I remember parts of Atlantis and how we lived. We operated under one universal law. It saddens me that people lost touch with their oneness. We have truly have been in the dark spirit ages, the ages of separation. We were at one point of our existence operating as one. We had no idea who we used to be as humans, that is until we get our memory back or until the awakening happens to each person one by one. It is our path to enlightenment not just mine. It is happening to each person one by one, we, you, are indeed headed into the realms of the light. In that light as we once were we lived a much different existence and let me remind you of that existence. This is an existence that you yourself may even have had a glimpse of or a memory of. I myself have a very fond profound memory of this; this is why I continue to work for Spirit as a messenger. We were (are) one and each of us knew it. We operated highly on energy. Everything was energy. I could see the energy fields around your body and I could sense and feel what was in your heart and mind, therefore we never crossed another's path; we would never. Light Workers are doing this here now! We are returning! Your energy showed everything about you as did mine. We knew who to do business with and who resonated with what we wanted. Not only were we telepathic-energy-sensitive beings, we were beings that were so sensitive to the energy around us that we collectively controlled the weather.

We recognized that we were one with the elements and the elements that surrounded and moved with our sacred planet swarmed and moved with our sacred bodies, and we were indeed not only in control of our inner climate and our inner health, we collectively had control over the elements as we were all one with everything~~*Everything that is my child everything, everything you see is a divine construct of everything. You are in the individual form of me for there was no separation; there is no separation between me and that beautiful tree you see sitting outside your window. There is no separation between the bum you see on the street and me; there is no separation between the articles you see in your room for there is no separation from the Divine. What may I ask you are you doing with me? What are you doing with me my children, for I am here to check on you now? Where have you been; what have you been doing with this body of light I have given you of mine, my child, for I am so anxious to see your world. Please show me and prepare for me what you have made for me. I want to see you. I want to see all your magnificent creations, what will you show me my dear soul. What can the "I" that "I" am" experience through you and only you for you are my master? What shall we prepare today?, My child, tell me. For you are never without me. Literally everything you see you are one with. Everything you see is one with the atom and cells in your body, everything. Do not think for one minute you are separate from anything you see, for I tell you are not. Everything you see is alive. Not only is everything alive, it is looking back at you. It is alive because you make it alive by observing it. Once you have observed something, you have literally brought it into existence. Make no mistake you are a Creator beyond what you have remembered. Everything is alive. When you understood this; you understood your oneness with all creation. There is no sickness in the mind that you are, for there is no lack of our oneness, for you reside in the eternal moment of now with heightened states that are in union with me that allows one's chi to restore all illness.*

One's chi is restored because in the meditative states you remembered how and you remembered your glory and restored your Chakras therefore restoring any discord in the physical and or spiritual centers. You lived for thousands of years and were the Creator of your dominions. You created for me and you called it good. You called it what you wanted because you created what you wanted, for you were in full remembrance of your brilliance with me and in your brilliance with me there was no lack, no limitation, no discord, no disease, no mental illness, no need for drugs, no need for separation. Although you my child have chosen to separate, you have lost your memory of your grandness. For all the attributes of what you have known to be of God are also the attributes that lie within you. Right here right now within you are the keys to the entire universe. Though my largeness is farther than what your mind can imagine, make no mistake the entire existence of the Universe resides right in your one-person, seemingly small being. For within a mustard seed you shall also see the entire realms of existence there, is no separation. The microcosm the macrocosm we are divinely connected to it all~~

This is my memory, imagine everyone remembering this. For we are remembering this, each of us, you, me, your pain, my pain, the changing of the planet, the prophesies, the directions the animals are taking, the centers of our brains awakening, all this and so very much more shows us we are all awakening. For your pain and my pain has never gone without purpose, that there is a savior coming and the savior is happening within you and within me and that God itself hears and feels every waking glorious part of it. You are part of it; I am part of it and it is indeed happening.

REALITY TODAY

When my life unraveled itself to me and I became aware of the higher dimensions, it was then made clear to me that I was to be a Light Worker, that what I had been through brought me to the higher realms of existence and therefore I was to be a messenger and spread the good news. I see that we are more. I hear that we are more and I prove it. All people that know they are Gods have an opportunity to bring this action forth and prove it for themselves. I will tell you to the end of my days we were meant to be Gods. We are literally the sons of a God, as earth herself was birthed out of glory, and to glory it will return. You have in your DNA the genetic code to become aware that you are a God. There was never meant to be this poverty this sickness this hated this robbery, we were Gods of a very large kind.

We were all God-Like beings of a supreme kind. Do not be mistaken of this. This is the message to penetrate into your being. This is the message you cannot forget; this is the message sent to us over and over through our ascended masters. The message doesn't change, but people have changed the message. Our scriptures were burned at the libraries of Alexandria but the message has remained. It remains because it is within us. It remains because it remains in the DNA molecules in our bodies and within the planets that are electromagnetically connected to our subtle energies that surround our body through our Chakra centers. Ascended Masters are very well aware how to use and maneuver these energies and that is why they are able to perform such miracles such as Jesus, Yizzu, Joshua. We have the same capabilities deep within us to be restored. You can replenish your chi over and over and over if needed. In other civilizations we can sleep or not. In fact, it is rare to sleep or eat; both are very dense to lighter beings. In fact, many on earth have tapped into the centers that I have now and understand the concept of solar chi or food from Source. These Breatha-terians have not had food or drink for years. As of now there are approximately 45,000 around the world as I write this, (reference Jashmuheen) although with the planetary changes the rate of this is evolving very fast. One will tap into the Avatar of their higher being, the same being that is within each of us. Our bodies as a whole were meant to be magnificent for years. Imagine just getting out of adolescence at fifty to seventy years of age. I am not kidding; this is also the average age of starting adulthood in other civilizations.

A Light Worker named Skye

We are so engrossed with things we call food it is no wonder so many are crippled. We are engrossed with TV reality shows that are reaping ego. Everyone loves the "ideal" thing but behind the ideal is a person that you labeled less than the other, and this is not accurate; accurate is being better than you used to be; it has nothing to do with the other person but let's rip up anything pure and natural and authentic. We send thousands to Hollywood to become stars of the ego. The ego that says that there is someone who looks better has better and is better, and we spend a lifetime trying to prove something we almost believe in. People spend their money, their lives, their heritage their sanity trying to prove to be more, as if you could be more then you already are. They slave at jobs they really don't even believe in to have everything show up a certain way in the outer world that would somehow prove their importance. It is a façade and it is a joke to the human reality of our heart. We are growing, and we are all able to see past this artificial state being. On and on and on people work to have that name that will make them stand out from the rest as if there need to be more. In many higher civilizations you do not even have a name. More is the sickness and the separation from Source itself, and may I reassure you this is an endless pit of the ego to nowhere. I find people everywhere who have these real great homes but are never there to enjoy it because they are working their asses off for it. Therefore the house becomes the higher power. It's the outside shell that says you have become something to everyone else. The bigger it is the more you are as a person. That could not be any further from the truth. This gigantic space everyone believes they need is just more space to clean to me, unless it is a big house to help nurture the community and doing something to profit society. Big houses are great. We can do great work in them and express ourselves. Although I would say most people are unhappy and in over their heads to maintain slavery. I do not call this freedom.~~*You want to find wealth, find your heart and my dearest child make no mistake the riches of the kingdom will be added unto you far, far, far greater then you could even almost imagine.*~~This mentality of separation has deprived us from every God-given right and ability that we have.

I continue to know now after my intense continued work with the "Light Beings" that at one time we had full memory of our oneness and we will indeed return to this. We will be operating in a much greater state here on Planet Earth. We, you, and I are a God. We are a God of a very large kind, and we have had our memory erased. We have been deceived by the delusions of the world, and I am here to tell you there is more. There is more than growing up in a world where we suffer terribly over the loss of our children into the desperate hell one experiences. There is more than having an Archon or lower forms of energy running our bodies, our beings, and our planet. There is a way out from the Archons, too, yes, for they would not be in existence if there wasn't a way out. There is a yin to every yang and there is a yang to every yin. No, we are meant to experience so much more in this presence we call life. And the good news is we will. For the Supreme is not a wimp. If all we think we have is this life to relate to and that there are not realms or time lines where things are different or play out differently, we have not opened our third yet, know that you can also experience those timelines. There are many mansions in the kingdom. You are only experiencing one element of your entire existence and please do not get caught in the moment, that is unless you chose to. This Universe is far, far, far greater than what you have experienced, for you have not been privy to the other realms of existence that you are awakening to as your memory has been shut off when you agreed to be here with the rest of the planet. It is being restored every minute of your awakening now. *~~For your child is your greatest gift to find your way back home as your child's greatest gift to him or her was the drugs. For let duality serve its purpose, for you will all return to the light and live forever. For I have never ever left you, only your memory of me has left. Remember me contemplate what it was like to be with me. What was it like to see me in all you do? What was it like? Think back, remember being with me! Tell me, please tell me, I want to know you. I want to know all of you, for only through you can I exist. Prepare the way my child for I am here, I am here, I am right here—what are you doing with me?~~*

PART THREE-
ENLIGHTENMENT

CHAPTER 25

ENLIGHTENMENT;
LIFE ON ATLANTIS AND LEMURIA

Enlightenment has made its presence known in my life by surfacing its head through my emotional pains and is being used as a means to my awakenings in life. I must admit, as I never wanted to accept my pain meant anything but punishment, I now bravely call my emotional and spiritual deaths my resurrections and my enlightenment!.

Enlightenment. There is no other essence like this, and it is attainable to everyone according to my interpretations. Krishna, Buddha, and Jesus's (one of the same in mission) teachings have all made this clear to us. In scriptures—the Vedic writings one of the most ancient scriptures known to mankind, written around 3800 BC—as well as countless masters, ascended masters, and teachers have all made this clear.

The Sumerians as well as the Vedic texts also left us much information on our galactic families. I remember when I first had my encounter with the "Light Beings." I had shortly after met up with the Swami down the street at the Vedic center. I wanted to see what was going on with me and if these ET contact situations I was finding myself attuned to were real. I thought maybe he would be the person I could trust who could let me down gently. What he told me was I had better get lots of rest because what I was dealing with was probably very real. As he firmly nodded his head, "Yes, yes, you will need rest." Later, I understood what he really meant. "At the time," I said, "all I do is have energy," which is true after a Kundalini awakening; a burst of energy comes forth as one automatically places oneself in their "Dharma." Though, every time an upgrade happens, or a strong vibration comes in from another dimension of such high vibration, there is an adjustment that takes places in the "contactee's" body.

Many contactees experience physical symptoms at various degrees when they are upgrade or attuning. Some of them include dizziness, ringing in the ears, faint, tired heart palpitations. Rest is needed. Dolores Cannon had spoke of this as well.

No matter where the message comes from or how it travels here to our dimension, the message doesn't change. Enlightenment: it is attainable to all (in fact, meant for all), and it is meant for all of time. It is a state of being I would describe as attunement. We lived like this on Earth before, and most of our galactic family always lives like this in their civilizations. We lived like this in Atlantis and Lemuria. These civilizations lived in supreme glory and oneness before their destruction.

When I truly touch supreme energy and spend a minute there without interpreting it, I burst into tears. For its energy of love will burst and purge out of me thoughts in my energy field that are anything unlike itself, that self that is complete "Love." It is the vibration of love, acceptance, and peace. It is superior in its healing and manifestation qualities. We used its energy as if it were fuel. In fact, it was our fuel. It is how we managed our Merkaba, the energy field around us, the literal energy that can pick our essence up, and move it from one place to another in its full usage.

Peace. There is nothing like this peace. If I could give a gift to the world, it would be this peace I found in enlightenment. The entity known to be Joshua (aka Jesus) has been known to state this at the Last Supper. My peace I leave you. He knew the glory of the Father within (in Heaven). Many masters have become masters enduring horrible lives giving messages of love regardless. I now understand the drive and the longing these entities had to portray these messages. When you touch enlightenment, ironically enough, you would die for it. We do, in fact, the death of the Egoic Mind takes places right before enlightenment.

On this journey we are all taking, one comes to understand this type of Enlightenment through ironically dating the dark. Dating, going out with, learning about or full on encountering the dark in life, as we are beings of both light and dark. All energies on this planet exist and operate over a yin-yang principle. Up-down, hot-cold, male-female, dark-light; we agreed to live on a planet of polarities.

Chapter 26

The Divine Mother... the Beings Continued Communication on How to Cope on Earth

As I have stated throughout this book, I clearly and graciously say to you that during all my life's challenges, alongside of me, I have paid attention to that loving voice that remains inside all of us. I call it Source and I call it "Divine Mother's voice." The Female voice of Source. Within each of us is a male and female God, a right and left brain Shiva, Shakti. This voice has been a voice of gentle wisdom to me in the darkest nights of my soul. I have needed this light. I could not have survived without this. Its presence was like a gift to me when I felt it. My channels are much more open now a days to source because of the years of pain blowing them open. It is connected to me now as part of my makeup. I constantly feel Source. I feel the flutters on my face and the tapping on my nose often these days. Especially when I ask questions. I have tendencies to ask.

Source today is a oneness that divided into an individual called me, whereas before it was more of something outside of me I prayed to, thinking if I was good enough I would have its benefits, not knowing its perfect beauty was inside of me right here and right now. Regardless of my level of understanding or not, its essence remains real and effective.

A Light Worker named Skye

Regardless of me leaving it or not, it has always been there and never has left my side. Although, I have left it and its knowledge often. There are even times I felt like it bugged me when it first started. I was getting massive messages that there were going to be changes on the planet through the ETs/ Light Beings. I was even starting to tell people before I even knew what I was talking about, so it all sounded weird, and of course everyone else thought it was weird as well when I talked about it. Those persistent beings didn't seem to mind. They just kept contacting me in all kinds of interesting ways, especially in the astral realm and in dreams. Interestingly, it was all at the height of Lara's illness, and that is where my mind was, not on these strange things that, one day, might come about. I had no mental room, I guess. That's why I didn't think it was important or going to be so accurate one day because it was so farfetched. Nowadays the communication is so vibrant. It became even more accurate as time went on. It became clearer. The kinetic connection was really what caught my attention. The taps or flutters on the nose or face became more direct and distinct. I knew when it was Creator God as opposed to the taps from and ascended master or an ET Family, or Mother Earth herself.

It's given me the ability to read it, to read the "universal truths;" universal truths that we all operate on within our Galactic family. In other civilizations, as I stated, they operate under the "Law of One." Our planet and this dimension, the third dimension, is going to be raised to the fourth and fifth dimensions. As our planet continues to shift, we will learn quickly that you only function under the "Law of One." All beings adhere to this in the outer galaxies and in those kinds of dimensions.

I read our oneness. This light comes in many forms to me but, usually, is hovering in thought-form around something (could be anything). Many times, I can read it so clearly. I am telling you it is the most beautiful language I have ever connected with. When I feel a touch, a light-vibration touch that confirms it is light or a presence connecting to me from the Angel/ET/Ascended Master realm(s), I am instantly comforted. I remember I am not alone in the days and nights I suffer over my daughter. Your not alone either, you might not know it yet, but you will. Use my faith if you ever lose yours.

There is also on occasion a popping noise that comes from the crown of the head when I am connected to the divine. I, however, never limit how the connections are made, because the ultimate Creator is not limited to form or non-form. It is form and formless and communicates in all ways and in more than one way, as creation should and does. It is our filters that need to be cleaned in order to perceive such greatness from the higher realms that we all have access to.

Everything is much more complex than something we just hear (as in through our ears). One of the first things I mentioned in one of my videos was that our senses are our limitations. They constrict things into what we see with the two eyes and not the third and what we hear in our outer world. Sources message surpasses the understanding of religions, for it does not get caught up in repeating scriptures or doctrine nor limits itself to not speaking through religions, scriptures, or sections of worship.

I've again surrendered to the fact that I am never going to fully explain this. Wisdom gently reminds me that I don't have to. So, I drift off with that nature. Either I will be heard, or I won't, but what I do know is that if a soul is in need of a message, and it is open to its answers, those answers will come to that person, whether through my interpretation, through a writing piece, or through someone or something else, but rest assured, a message will be sent to whomever asks, and all answers are sent as well.

Something very interesting has also been made aware to me by the light. It was its gift to me from Source (itself) as promised in the beginning. Source made deals to me too that it was intending to keep. I did not know that. Love has intended, all along, to come back to us, to once again make itself known to our planet. Make no mistake, I have been shown we are in the times now, and entering into the times now where we are going to see the return of love on our planet. Yes, there are going to be changes on our planet beyond what we can imagine when love returns. Though, let's not forget that love is always here where we are right now.

We, ourselves, are separated from Source on our own, and it is our responsibility to get back. We were never alone. Our child is exactly where he/she is supposed to be, whether we see past the appearance of it or not and whether or not we are part of the picture or not, since this is, indeed, his/her own soul journey and its mission. Point blank: I am quite certain my daughter would be on her mission with or without me.

I stood before this light everyday when I begin to write to you and with you. Sometimes, I worry about what it says because it makes such bold statements that unravel the thread of our existence and how we relate to the world. This voice gently reminds me that if I have the balls to let it work through me, then I had better stand back and not edit its voice any more than my personal human filters do. My job is to be a channel period. Why me? Why this? Why such pain over my child? I ask this "Mother's Divine voice." It just gently spoke and speaks regardless of how much pain I was in throughout my writings. "Get up girl. Get up, because no one's pain on this planet has ever been without a purpose and not one single prayer that has been placed on its altar has ever gone unheard."

This was also not just about me here. This was about all human suffering. My daughter's illness and the captivation from the Archons, the devastation that has dropped me to my knees, has been the same devastation that pushed me over the edge in life enough to do something about it. I'd like to boldly call this the "final devastation" that made me surrender my beliefs from the world as I have learned it to be, the world of illusions, the Matrix, as I talk about also in my videos that I continue to make and to start opening my mind to an entirely different world, the world of loving universal truth where we all meet as one, OUTSIDE the Matrix. That same hell you fell into (if you are the parent of an addict with mental illness or the parent of a child with an Archon taking over or electronic energy or just plain in hell from the Archon Network) is the exact hell that will raise you to your peace of mind beyond what you ever knew. **We must strive to use our pain as a gift to search for further answers to our freedom out of the illusions of the world.** We must no longer be held captive by our fears that the lower worlds have held us under.

The planets and our evolving consciousness will not tolerate it now. We have suffered enough, to be caught in such illusions of the world. The false belief that we are separate from each other must be shattered in order for us to raise our standards to the levels that are being asked of us. Especially now, there are going to be massive changes on our earth, as I continue to state. My readings of the current vibrational pole on our planet is that we are now, each of us, truly headed upward to higher evolved states of being. We, as humans, are heading into advanced states of being. Though, we are going to go through massive birthing pains. When I say our planet is not going to tolerate this that is exactly what I mean. Mother Earth is changing and evolving. Her DNA is changing. Therefore, we are going to be changing as people. The Sun is literally sending us signals of this brilliance. The Sun has its own direction, its own course, and even the new Second Sun we will soon hear more about. Parents that are in this situation are highly evolved souls, in preparation for this journey that is happening on our planet. THE NEW PARADIGM.

Prior to tapping into any of the higher realms in life, I was in no way able to cope with what was in front of me. In fact, I wasn't coping at all. I was dying. I was feeling my essence slowly drift weaker and weaker, as if the emotional life was being sucked out of me, straight to the nothingness. By higher realms, I do not mean just a higher power. I am talking about tapping into using the spiritual higher centers of our being that teaches and shows us perspectives that makes all of this nonsense make sense. It is also the centers that allow us to understand and compact the Archon Network as a whole; tapping into the highest centers of your being where you are able to tap into your psyche, your physical body, and your emotional centers, to repair any damage you have acquired during the days of terrifying worry, extreme stress, insomnia, and all the aspects that come with having your life terrorized, going through it all. Yes, we are able to have complete mental, physical, and emotional freedom, to restore our bodies and our essence back to new as if we had never been harmed.

Chapter 27

My First Translation from the Light Beings....
~The Death of the Egoic Mind~

I have come to understand that all mankind, that is, every soul being will have "THE DEATH OF THE EGOIC MIND;" the reckoning of the soul; the dark night of the soul in order for a true awakening to occur. Each soul, whether conscious of this or not, is on a journey back to the Supreme. We are on an evolutionary planet. Everything that is happening or not happening is a design to get us back to reunite and cleanse us of the original separation from Source. Source is where all things come from; Love energy; Free energy for the Planet; Light; Supreme states of existence. Before we were dummied down as a culture and separated from Source, as I have explained quite a bit, we lived in a state of supreme existence, on many levels and in many forms. We lived like Gods. We, through time, a long time, have separated ourselves to such extreme levels that we did not even know we were separate. The pain is the call back to the supreme state of existence. That is why the pain is so intense. It is designed to knock us off our feet and into the higher realms.

We want to solve problems for our children based on the human mentality that, of itself, is lost in a virus of a spiritual kind. Truth is not at the level of the egoic mind where we are aimlessly trying to get answers. We want answers from the lower realms of the third-dimensional world. The higher realm of the enlightenment is where one can see the perfection in all situations and all situations regarding our son's or daughter's life. The egoic thought systems must be destroyed in order to obtain freedom from the lower levels of the excruciating pain, worry, devastation, and heartache we repeatedly experience.

The time has come on our planet where the egoic mind is being destroyed. One by one, event by event, disaster by disaster, people are laying down their arms to a humanity that is surrendering and wanting more. As I have been stating the planet's evolving consciousness will not tolerate lower levels of thought forms. The planet, meaning me, meaning us, meaning Mother Earth "Gaia," is evolving. At the center of the galaxy, the planets and our Sun (or the Son connected to the Most High) are aligning, literally, with the rest of the Galaxy and all its wonder. That literally means we are changing as a culture and as humanity the same way the earth's DNA is changing. Don't forget we are all connected in the microcosmic and macrocosmic scheme of things. The universe and the planets and stars that orbit around the sky in a perfect order and fashion is also rotating and designed the same way inside the center of our brains, in perfect order and fashion. Our heart's oracles are the same heart oracles of the earth, as indicated in our sacred structure in the Oracle of Delphi. The rotation in our eyes and our pupils will match the universe. There is no separation. Mother Earth has energy vortexes around her the same way we have our seven Chakra vortex centers. Our bodies are designed in perfect relation to everything that exists. In all things, from little to astronomical, we recognize our oneness.

Our essence and our lives will crumble without facing the demons that are pulled out of our own skin over our sons or daughters. It is by design that we are chemically wired to our offspring, and it is our powerful Mother Nature instinct to protect. Science proves our children have their very own stems cells that, although in a separate body, are the offshoot of ours. Therefore, we are biologically wired to each other. It has been proven many times in my case when Lara and I were living together during her younger years. I always knew when it was time to change her diaper even when I wasn't there. I sensed her needs as if it were my own body. We hear countless references to mothers who just knew something was going on with their child. They just knew. When I awaken the cells within my body, I literally awaken the cells within her, that is how divinely connect we are.

A Light Worker named SKYE

This planet has been infected by a very serious human virus of what, as I mentioned, Source and the Light Beings call the "Egoic Mind," the mind of duality and the world of illusions. I am going to repeat here as it is needed. Most of us are walking around blind, not knowing how truly hypnotized we have been from the truth of our being. We are not just lost in the Matrix, we are truly lost in a **controlled** Matrix. We must obtain freedom from our erroneous thoughts of the world and what we think the world should look like in order to unbrainwash us from the lies infested in humanity, freedom from the erroneous messages given to us derived from years and years of a controlling fear-based thought system(s) that have been running on our planet. Messages that are so deeply engrained in the fabric of our brains that we do not even recognize them as erroneous. Almost everything we communicate to each other is based in the world of illusions.

I felt a deep responsibility and sadness for my daughter's illness, and I was on a deep mission to cure it. I reviewed everything over and over. I persecuted myself, and I must tell you that Spirit stopped me. It was and is and will remain the drive behind my writings. I say to myself over and over how can I sit here and blame myself and blame my daughter when I sit here and realize we are all in the world of illusions.

Source continues as it immediately stops me and sets off speeding out of me my first direct unedited translations about the EGOIC MIND and what it means (this is what the darker energies are, Gods of, on our planet, per our permission):

~ Predominately, media as projections of your world through news, beauty images, false competitions, misinterpretations of illness and disease. Predominately, mass corporations controlling your subconscious through advertising as means to control. Predominately, religions controlling through fear. Predominately, school systems in every country teaching government curriculums rather than truth. Predominately, financial systems where money is used as a means of trade, giving money itself false power rendering it your God's. Predominantly judicial systems that promote a right and wrong system based on false concepts of right and wrong. Using methods of rehabilitation in prison systems that breeds more dysfunctions. Predominantly, belief systems that put one against the other or make another appear better. Belief systems that suggest there is only one way rendering another less. Predominantly misguided priorities where

My First Translation from the Light...

individuals are targeted to advance rather than the whole. Things that are anything unlike THE LOVELY SPIRIT SELF and its natural state of love that is your true nature ~...

Many now, on our planet during this new consciousness shift, are being called to awaken. Many are awakening to the truth. It doesn't take a genius to see and understand the violence we live in is not human nature. I believe many people are awaiting a second coming of some kind, a return of the God(s) and the God within, and are now being called to prepare for the arrival of freedom. Every day I wake up, my first aim is to be aware of the illusions of the world. How each of them must be shattered in order for me to gain complete clarity on how to handle what is in front of me with a higher source rather than the limited access that one attains through thought systems already in place from outside sources or the lower consciousness thought realms. Before we even had a chance to think for ourselves, we were made to have certain information drilled in our heads, so young, and all for a reason. It is literally controlled to the extent whereas if you do not obtain this information, then you are considered a lower member of society and are alienated. If we do not follow programs given to us from society, government(s), and religion(s), then we are alienated from society for not agreeing.

I feel a big responsibility for Lara's illness, but today, it is not because I am desperately lying on the ground with guilt as a mother. It is because of the world I brought her into. I brought her into a world that has a human virus, controlled by the dark. There was very little defense against this at that stage of the game until I myself started healing the human virus by healing myself and my attachment to the virus. This, I felt, I owed my daughter. This, I realized through my daughter, I owed myself. This, I also realized, I owed the planet. I was taken out of the Matrix without asking. I was permitted to see the truth. There is no separation between me, you, and Prime Creator. With the information I had, it was no longer acceptable for me to walk around in the egoic mind of the Matrix, nor could I.

Once it became clear to me that spirit has guided and driven my heart to wake up from the world of illusions (my purpose in everything I do), I became direct and targeted with guidance and fire. Once you surrender from the world of illusions or the "Death of the Ego" miracles fly through your system fast. You will be guided without mistake when and where and how you need to be for the greatest good of yourself and the greatest good for your child. Especially now, the spirit source within desires to wake up entirely and the planets are lining up to do so. In the name of spirit, you will have all power for manifestation. This was how it was intended. In spite of your doubt, pull your mind's power back to your third eye, back to your pineal gland. Meditate through this place rather than what you are seeing with your outer eyes. Truth will be shown to you through these centers. These centers are the storing house for truth. When raising our energy through meditations, all Chakras align, offering accurate information from each particular center, which is stored in our third eye centers (or our pineal gland). This is the source of all information.

Source channels me strongly forth:~~~*The reason we are ever so deeply affected by something in the first place is because there are erroneous messages somewhere along the way in our internal being that believe things must turn out a certain way in order for one to call it okay. This is where your pain originates. You have your view of what you think, not only you but how another should show up in the world. The problem is, this configuration you have made up for each of yourselves is not of your true selves. Slow down for a moment your idea of who you have placed yourself to be in your current state. Let the concept of just your personality start to fade off from your thought system. Continue until a clean state of, "no personality." You are no longer who you identify with. You are just you, with no outside story of who you think you are. No identity. No attachment to a person or place. Just you. Take a moment in that clear space. Who are you? Are you believing what you yourself have found to be truth or are you believing what you believe you are supposed to believe? Who has dictated to you who you are in your world? Do you agree with this dictation? Have you ever stopped to think of who is the self you are agreeing with or is this a "self-made" being from an outer world rather than inner?~~*

Now we have ideas for ourselves that are put into our brains from an outside world we believe to be credible. We believe all the information to be credible without ever checking its message until our higher self is brought to the surface for clarification. One by one, illusion by illusion, the world of illusions will tear itself down before us, tear by tear as we slowly surrender from the way we think life should be according to what we have been told or what we have fantasized.

My First Translation from the Light...

We surrender our erroneous thoughts and illusions of the world. We lay these erroneous messages we have learned about ourselves and our loved ones before the fire to burn. We understand that they, too, are brought up in the world of illusions and are fighting their own battle of illusion. We free ourselves beyond recognition. We stand with all power. You are powerful beyond what you know when your illusion of your lower worldly self has been destroyed. We stand before our centers with a clear state of mind. We continue to tear down the illusions we have placed on others as we have ourselves. We step outside the Matrix. Source continues, *~~If each person were operating from within their true selves rather than the dummy versions we have all assigned each other and ourselves, there would only be each person living from the center of God-essence; the heart center. If each person were living from the center of self then your world would be a world of love and nothing other. Love resides in the center of your hearts. When each person is operating from the center of their heart they have entered the Tone of Oneness. When you are in the vibration of our oneness, you, I, the all, we are automatically operating in sync with all of nature and all of its sentient beings allowing each person to flow perfectly in sync with the others operating outside the Matrix, allowing only love to rule. Imagine what your world would be like, like this. No, imagine here, right here, right now, imagine, then imagine some more. Your imagination is where I take my first breath with you. Breathe more my child, breath me in, breath my breath, your imagination is where I lie, my child of light, imagine my light through your breath, breathe my light in your being through your imagination. I am...imagination, breathe me in, let your body feel the vibration of our oneness and spark it with the fire it was meant to have. Take this powerful energy and let it blast through your being, penetrating it through any erroneous thoughts you had about yourself and any separation you may have had from your Ultimate Creator God. Let it cleanse you, let it cleanse your very being, your heart your mind and your body. This is now your purification into the realms of any corner of your being that was ever harmed in ANY WAY, from the hell you have taken on from loving an addict and thereafter. Stay here with me a minute, breathe me, feel the me you were meant to have, all the love, all the glory, all the peace, all the contentment I am, the I am, that I am, is you. Take this fire and spark and light that I am* *through you and place it in your home, from your home, place it in your city, and from your city, to your country, from your country to other nations, from other nations to the planet to Gaia to the galaxies and back to self...May you understand that your word is my command. Thank you for letting me service you and cleanse your mind body and spirit as you now have done.~~*

63465023R00126

Made in the USA
Lexington, KY
07 May 2017